The
Sales Professionals'
Master Workbook of
S.Y.S.T.E.M.S

(Saving You Stress, Time, Energy, Money & Sleepless Nights)

Gerard Assey

The Sales Professionals' Master Workbook of S.Y.S.T.E.M.S
By
Gerard Assey
© Copyright 2020 by Author

Published by:
Gerard Assey
19/18, Palli Arasan Street
Anna Nagar East
Chennai - 600 102

ISBN: 978-81-946847-5-6

Cover Design & Layout:
Kulothungan G,
Chennai - 600 044

CONTENTS

DEDICATION

This book: 'The Sales Professional's Master Workbook of S.Y.S.T.E.M.S' is lovingly dedicated to ' *The Great Name, Above All Names, The God of the Impossible, The One and Only One'* Who has blessed me beyond imagination.

A work of this nature can never be accomplished purely by the efforts of one person. It often is the culmination of a progressive learning process-firstly through my own experience in Sales and Management, through trial and error, along with the many people in my working career, coupled with the many courses, books/ videos/ CD's that have also significantly impacted my life.

Consequently, some of the ideas involving the skills & techniques reflect the concepts that I have internalized which we use in our programs

To all my clients, customers, sales personnel and associates that worked with me and taught me the numerous lessons- A BIG Thanks!

And finally to you my reader- Thank you for obtaining this copy! I have done my part. Now it is your turn to apply these concepts by putting it to practice!

We both need each other!

"...But those who hope in ADONAI will renew their strength, they will soar aloft as with eagles' wings; when they are running they won't grow weary, when they are walking they won't get tired" **Isaiah 40:31 (CJB)**

FOREWORD

I am privileged to write this foreword for this meticulously compiled one stop manual for a Sales Professional by my friend and colleague Gerard Assey - a brilliant sales person himself. If you have bought this book, let me assure you, that it has all there is to learn about consultative selling!

I met Gerard way back in 1987 when both of us joined an organisation that shaped our careers in sales and firmly got us hooked to selling as a profession - and it soon became a way of life. The learning's from that stint at GETIT yellow pages built several careers in sales for fresh, enthusiastic youngsters that have never looked back since. I went on to become the Managing Director of an American Hospitality multinational for their South Asia operations and several of our colleagues too climbed the corporate ladder swiftly - armed with the ability to be able to close deals. We were bound by that one thread - our passion for consultative selling!
The key to this form of sales is to completely understand the current and future needs of your prospective customer and then make a bespoke recommendation to enable her to make an informed buying decision. This is easier said than done! It requires tremendous amounts of patience, empathy, restraint, sensitivity and squeaky clean ethics. All of us human beings can sell at one level or the other, which is why you were hired in the first place. But a Master sales person is one who can do it with panache in a manner that is non-threatening and keeps the customer engaged throughout an extended period of time.

Gerard is an absolute STAR salesperson with huge doses of each of the attributes mentioned above. This amazingly structured book he has put together, with his long years of experience both on field as a sales professional, and as a coach and mentor for several sharp minds across the world will bring out the best in you.

Just go get that sale!!!

Radhika Shastry
(Former Managing Director),
RCI-South Asia

"In a highly competitive field, today's sales professionals approach is mostly driven by the market forces or competition. This often is counterproductive and leads to his failure. Gerard has tried to address this in his book which helps a sales professional remain organised and optimise his skills. Coming from a master who has headed highly disciplined and competent sales teams, the book is timely and bound to be a big hit"

- A.M. Sundar,
CFO & Company Secretary, SNOWMAN LOGISTICS LIMITED

"Interesting narrative on the sales process in the changing markets , a practical and an implementable one; if practiced well, can add value to both corporates and the customer. A must read for a budding professional and to the seasoned ones to re-visit basics like never before."

-Raja Rajasekar K S,
Deputy General Manager-HR, KONE Elevator India Pvt. Ltd.

"For two decades of my professional life I have followed the principles of 'consultative selling', stretching the concept beyond sales to communication - this has contributed in a major way to successes along my career. I remember looking for guidance on how to improve my consultative selling skills and found none. Glad that Gerard's book is timely, especially since the field of 'sales' is not looked upon too kindly. By detailing a step-by step systematic approach on understanding client needs first and then working to meet these needs, the book is designed to nurture a 'sales professional persona' to mirror not just the brand or product, but also the company's image of 'customer first, product or service next'..."

-Sangeetha Rosemarie Rajeesh,
Research Uptake and Communications Manager,
Leveraging Agriculture for Nutrition in South Asia Consortium
M S Swaminathan Research Foundation

"Sales is considered one of the toughest jobs, but Gerard has made a step by step, structured approach to make this sales function as appealing and passionate..."

- Antony Prakash K,
Head & General Manager HR, CEAT LTD.

PREFACE

Thank you and Congratulations on obtaining a copy of this exciting book titled: **The Sales Professional's Master Workbook of S.Y.S.T.E.M.S'**, which has been designed exclusively for you- to help you be better at the job and more professional.

As you will notice later, after reading the book that the book is uniquely designed to help transform you into a Master Sales Consultant by helping you, discover the secrets that drive the top world's sales professionals.

It will help you or your team create the habits and lasting changes by enabling you replace current unacceptable patterns that are costing your company sales with new ones, that will now help you achieve your sales goals faster and more consistently

The entire book has been split into several step by step, easy and digestible modules, to help you take back and put to practice each step into a real life situation. That way these skills that you will learn will stay with you, enabling you to become more Professional and Successful in a sales role.

Interestingly, you will find that this entire program is suitable for anyone relatively new to selling, as well as, the more experienced ones, who wish to refresh or fine tune their existing skills, by giving it a more professional and systematic way of working, in line with today's' need for this type of Consultative or Relationship building approach.

Hopefully by the time you complete this entire program, it will benefit you in several ways...

Firstly, to ensure that you are equipped with the Professional Skills, that will not only help you in the business world, but on the Personal side as well. It will provide a step by step professional approach that will enable you take your customers through, to help them deal with you in ways, as you will see later, using a Consultative or Relationship building approach, thus leading to a lasting relationship. This in turn will help you and the organization you work for to obtain repeat business and referrals.

You will also find that after this session, you will be able to better manage yourself as well as be able to better manage your customers-both external as well as internal!

'The Sales Professional's Master Workbook of S.Y.S.T.E.M.S' will provide a very structured, formatted, step by step approach guiding even a novice as well as the most experienced Sales Person into Professionalism that will help '**win and keep customers for life**'!

You, the reader will be able to experience:

- *The benefits derived from the effectiveness of Consultative Selling and how different it is from the traditional sales approach,*
- *Learn how to guide prospects through the buying process*
- *Proven behaviors that make you stand out as a sales professional*
- *A thorough understanding of the Attributes and Activities of a Professional Sales Person*
- *Effectively prepare for any Sales Call*
- *Be able to manage your Time and Territory much better*
- *Build Rapport and Trust with a customer right during the approaching stage itself.*
- *Effectively uncover a customer's Needs, Problems and Opportunities and be able to demonstrate how your product features can help a customer meet a need/solve a problem (Proving Value).*
- *Be able to recommend an appropriate solution (Recommending) and Close business deals effectively after showing a customer how specific business objectives can be met and benefit by using your recommended product or service (Closing)*
- *Implement the entire consultative selling process into your daily work*
- *Most importantly, in every chapter or topic that is covered, there are several exercises for you to work on and put the new skills to immediate use.*

After reading the book, you will be able to gain a full understanding of both the buying and selling processes, including the importance of being well organized. And over the period, you would have worked through the Six Step Sales Process, practicing and mastering the skills at each stage, so that your selling skills are developed and reinforced

With no gimmicks, no jargon, just emphasis on relationship building, I believe that this is a well structured course on 100% building value and long lasting partnerships with your customer!

Before you move forward on this exciting journey that I am about to take you through, I would recommend that you have a note pad and pen to make notes of important points along with completing the exercises provided, that you can start using immediately.

So are you ready to embark on this exciting journey with me? Take your time, sit back & enjoy these learning's!

HOW TO GET THE MOST OUT OF THIS BOOK:

'The Sales Professionals' Master Workbook of S.Y.S.T.E.M.S'

1) Make a commitment to dedicate a fixed amount of time each day/ week: The results will depend on the time and efforts you put in to follow on the self-paced process that this book will take you through
2) Decide what you want to get out of this book- the objective and how you intend doing this?
3) You must decide initially to get out of your comfort zone if you are to experience success from this.
   Remember: *'If you continue to do what you've always done, you will continue to get what you've always got!'* If you are looking at different (better) results, you must then look at doing different things and different ways!
4) The road to success is already walked and laid out for you. Someone has already been through the *'School of Hard Knocks'*! You don't have to waste time re-inventing the wheel.
5) Put the ideas to immediate practice-Apply the ideas to your selling situation. No idea or concept is worth anything, if it cannot be applied to real situations. So applying these principles by putting them to immediate practice is the KEY! The book will help you translate the concepts into your own specific situations right away.
6) Work on expanding your knowledge: Do additional reading/ listening/ watching videos/ CD's ...whatever that can help you stay ahead!
7) Keep a record of your new learning's/ experience in using them and your accomplishments. This is YOUR own workbook...Go ahead scribble, make notes. The words you read are really nothing. It's what you work on as you go along and put to practice is what really counts. The Tools, Exercises and Checklists are designed to help you be more organized and sell more successfully.
8) Learn to share with others how these ideas have helped you: That way these new skills and techniques help get embedded in your system
9) Finally, learn to have fun with every progressive step!
10) Now Enough of Theory! Let's just start by putting it into Practice!

THE SALES PROFESSION!

Why it is the most Fascinating, YET most hated profession?

For many of you that have decided to make Sales as your career and for those already in it for a number of years, you would have already begun to realize that this is one of the most fascinating, rewarding and the fastest 'climb-up-the-ladder' professions. In fact the 'majority' of Chief Executives you see today that head organizations have mostly moved up from the sales rung.

Yet sadly, it is also the most hated profession worldwide. For many years I was inhibited about getting into the Sales Profession for various reasons, and always opted for a 'behind the scenes job'. I had always perceived a salesperson to be untrustworthy, that used high-pressure tactics. How sad that a group consisting of a good percentage of the working public is thought to be so! And I believe, I could have lost out on a lot because of that and it was only much later in life, after getting into it, (by chance, not choice), did I realize what a fascinating profession it is to be in and how much of a contribution a sales person makes to others- his customers, his family, his company, the industry, the economy...it can go on, as you will see soon.

Why is Selling such a Great Profession?

Selling is filled with great opportunities! Unfortunately, the profession is tarnished, with 9/10 using a very unprofessional approach. And we (even you and I are customers!) remember only the bad.

However, it is said that the average sales person keeps more than 30 people employed!

It is also the oldest and largest income group in the world (Why oldest? The very first humans- Eve sold the idea to Adam of having the Apple in the Garden of Eden!)

It is the only field where there is:

- No real need for qualifications (If you have it helps further!)
- Age is no asset or liability
- Men/ women regardless of previous experience or employment are motivated to get in
- A sense of pride: "I am a sales person"

- Impressive income- you write your own pay check-unlimited
- Fastest growth-unlimited opportunities
- Flexibility
- Independence
- Constant Recognition
- Travel
- People-networking
- Exposure
- Knowledge-self improvement/ updating of knowledge
- You have personal security- a future: May lose tangible wealth, but can regain all with proper attitude. You can always get back into this profession, even after few years of being out!
- Can be a good influence to others to improve themselves.
- Fun along the way

Just think of it: Our country and some of the other world powers wouldn't be great economies if it were not for some of the great sales people that make great sales every day!

How about the book that you hold in your hands? Ever wondered how it got so far?

It got there because thousands of sales people sold something.

Let us start from the scratch and see this book as an example!

In order for this book to exist, a sales person first had to sell seeds and fertilizers to a farmer. Then a sales person had to sell trees to a paper mill. For the trees to be harvested and cut down, someone had to sell logging equipment to a logging contractor. In order to get the logs to the paper mill, someone had to sell a special lorry or truck to transport them.

For a paper mill to exist, it takes an investment of several millions. Somebody had to sell the banks on the idea that this would be a good investment. Research indicates that for a paper mill to be built it takes about several sales calls, several proposals, and several sales closed, not forgetting a good number of sales cancelled too.

After the paper is manufactured, somebody had to sell the paper for this book to the printer. For this book to be printed, somebody had to sell the printer a Printing Press, someone a binding machine, someone a trimmer, someone a packing machine etc. Don't forget the design that went into this book and the equipment required for that.

The printing company would not be in business, if it were not for its sales team calling on publishing houses. A book like this would not exist if it were not for the sales efforts of people like YOU- the sales team!

Yes, nothing happens unless somebody sells something!!

Selling is a wonderful profession. Just think of some of the salespeople who were involved in selling the machinery for the paper mill or the printing equipment. Some of them could have made enough and more to buy a resort or even an island. Yes, great things happen when someone sells something and does it well.

Now think of the budgets to run huge sales forces, the laptops, the software, presentation equipment, air tickets, hotel stays, conference calls, meetings, incentives and sales leads to call on new prospects. Yes only in this profession can you create wealth and redistribute wealth.

The best part is that selling is one of the best performing arts. The best actors make their art disappear...the same is true with great sales people. They don't focus on selling, because people hate being sold by pushy sales people. Customers on the contrary love to buy from great sales people.

Great Sales people don't sell- they just help people get want they want...as this book does. Yes, I believe with all my heart that it will help you get what you want too!

As we've just seen-Everything starts with a Sale! Surveys reveal that 74 to 84% of all revenue is generated from a Sales Persons Activity.

So why then- when there is much good about this profession, why is it the MOST HATED Profession?

You don't have to look far- If you see the gates of some of the buildings (particularly in Asian Countries), you will find signs put up: 'SALESMEN NOT ALLOWED'. And at the side of these, you will also find another sign that goes like this: 'DOGS NOT ALLOWED'. Isn't this sad? Such a powerful profession that has been looked down by the general public! I have for a major part of my career been in this profession and it is really depressing seeing these signs.

The question now is: Why do most people generally hate or avoid sales people? Why is this profession so tarnished?

In a recent survey, customers cited 80 various reasons why they hated Sales People. We will not be getting into all the 80 reasons, but let us just look at the top 7 reasons:

Ranking no.1 was 'not listening' followed by 'talking too much!' I believe these two go hand in hand. How much better it would be if the Sales person just spent more time listening and the amount of information he or she would be able to gather by doing so.

Next on the list was a lack of product, market or industry knowledge, which has an effect on one's credibility to a great extent, leading to distrust. Studies reveal that Trust is the bond or cement to a lasting relationship.

Fourth on the list is a lack of Follow-up. In other words, promises and commitments never kept, or false promises provided, which again leads to effecting credibility and eventually creating distrust.

The 5th top reason is one of the attributes that I see very often from Sales people who would do whatever it takes to get that order or business, and this comes from an inner lack of confidence or belief in oneself, company, product or service, coupled with the lack of overall knowledge. This leads to the sales person having to now bluff his way, to get the sale....and again leading to effecting the credibility and trust between the buyer and seller.

One of the main reasons why a sale is lost is that the sales person failed to take time in understanding the needs of the customer- which is now our 6th reason of why customers hate sales people. We will cover a lot on this in a later chapter.

Finally, the 7th top reason why customers hate salesmen is that the salesperson cannot or refuses to take a 'no' for an answer. We must realize that not everyone out there can be your customer or that the 'would have been customer 'did not see value in your products or service. This is because the customer was pushed with the features of the service, instead of the sales person explaining the benefits of what the product or service would do for the customer and the ultimate benefit or value he would gain if he did so! We'll cover more on this too in a separate chapter later.

Remember, finally, that the profession that you are in is **an honorable profession** and the only way we can stand out and make a difference is to stay professional, by avoiding these annoying traits.

EXERCISE

Ask yourself (or maybe do it with someone who could provide you with honest feedback) and list down all the possible traits that you could sometimes be exhibiting unknowingly that can put customers off!

1.

2.

3.

4.

5.

6.

7.

8.

9.

10.

(Some examples to help you: *wrong or false commitments, pressurizing, unwilling to give customer a chance to talk- not listening, rattling off the features of your products without understanding customers need...*)

Note: After you have your list, make an Action plan with a time frame on eliminating these annoying traits

1.

2.

3.

4.

5.

6.

7.

8.

9.

10.

KEY ATTRIBUTES OF A PROFESSIONAL CONSULTATIVE SALES PERSON

We now know what customers hate about salespeople. Before we go any further, let us now look at what can create satisfied customers. With this understanding I am just trying to build a platform as to what would be required if we are to stand out as Professionals!

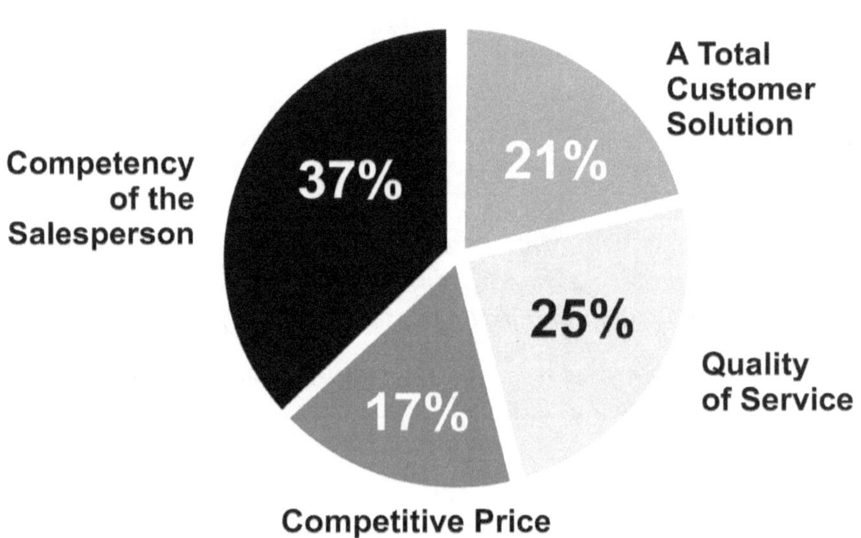

Illustration: 'What creates satisfied customers?'

According to another survey as you will see in the illustration, 37% has to do with the 'competency of the sales person', followed by 25% on the 'quality of product or service' provided. This was followed by 21% on the 'total solution' provided by the sales person or the right solution that matched the customers need and finally 17% had to do with a 'competitive rate or price'.

Now let us look at what is in your control as a sales person.
Is the competence of the sales person in your control....certainly a big YES!
Is the Quality of Service in your control....A big YES again!

A total Customer Solution...? Off course, without a doubt a big YES again.

And finally a Competitive Pricing...? Even if we are to say that this area lay with management or another department, you have a good 83% of what can create satisfied customers in your very control, so we as Sales People have no excuse in blaming anyone else when it comes to the dissatisfaction of customers.

We've just seen what creates satisfied customers....now taking this a little deeper on what the client specifically requires from your company that you represent, we can see that there are 4 vital areas:

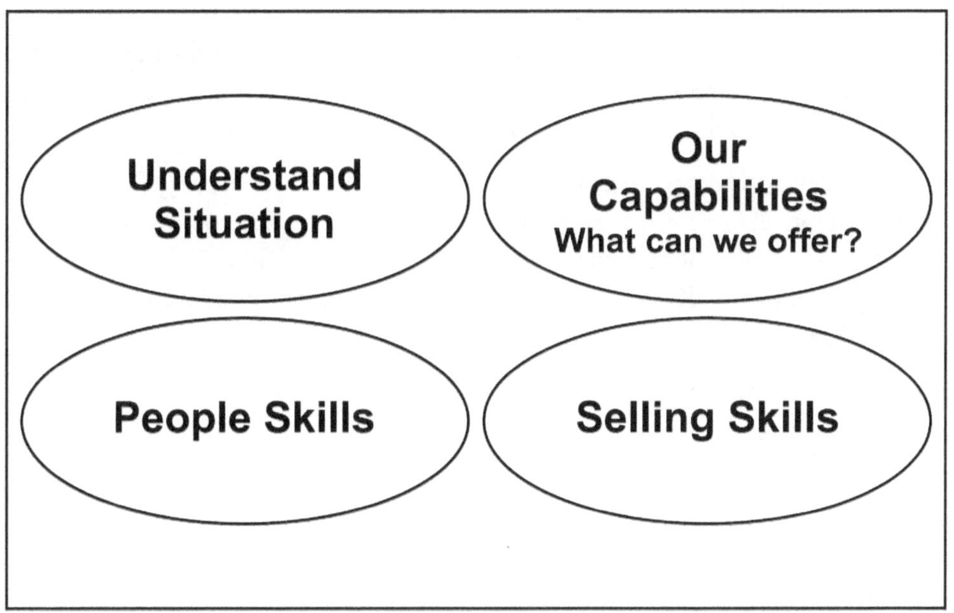

Illustration: What does client require from your company?

First and foremost is that:

Are we able to understand the situation of the customer, his specific needs, problems or pain areas? Are we more interested in helping him rather than just chasing for an order!

Second: would be on what have we got to offer that best matches that need that we've identified...in other words our capabilities. Have we been able to prove value of it?

How are you as a sales person, effectively going to use your skills to help him to buy; because people hate to be sold, they love to buy! In other words human beings love to own a decision for a good purchase they've made. This would be the Selling Skills part!

You are not pushing the customer, but you and the customer are working together as partners in taking a decision that can help the customer.

Finally, is the People Skills- meaning how effectively are you going to build a rapport and a long term relationship that can be a win-win situation for both the customer and your company. How courteous and friendly is your organization- especially when the customer does have a problem. Would your company be there when needed most?

We've just seen broadly what the client requires from you and your company. Now let us see what YOU as the salesperson will need to specifically have in order for you to achieve this objective.

While every business requires CASH to survive and succeed, every Professional Sales Person also requires something in them in order to succeed, which I believe is more valuable than that CASH. This is 'K.A.S.H.' because only when you have this KASH in you, you will be more successful in bringing in the CASH for you and your company.

So what is this KASH?

Knowledge

Attitude

Skills

Habits

Knowledge is all about your Company, the Products or Services that you offer, the Market and Industry that you operate in, together with knowing who are the other players or your competition that are in this industry. It also involves knowing where you stand against them-your strengths and areas that your competition has an advantage over you, along with being thorough on the rates, polices and regulations in your industry and market.

How effectively are you able to transfer this knowledge to the customer to enable him to deal or decide upon you as a service provider is a skill and the major part of this book is all about that.

Now there are various types of skill sets that people possess-

Eg; Selling Skills (the book in your hand incidentally is all about this),

Some other examples for Skills are:

Time Management

Team Working

Presentation Skills

Ability to present ideas in writing

Strategist- Prepares and Plans

Effective Communication

Negotiation Skills

Now having Knowledge and Skills alone is not enough. There are many sales people that have a great bank of knowledge along with the necessary skills, but yet have been total failures. Reason being they had a lousy attitude or very poor habits that killed a potential sale or the potential in them; that ultimately affected theirs and their organizations credibility

What you are seeing on the pie chart is the mental make-up of a Professional Sales Person.

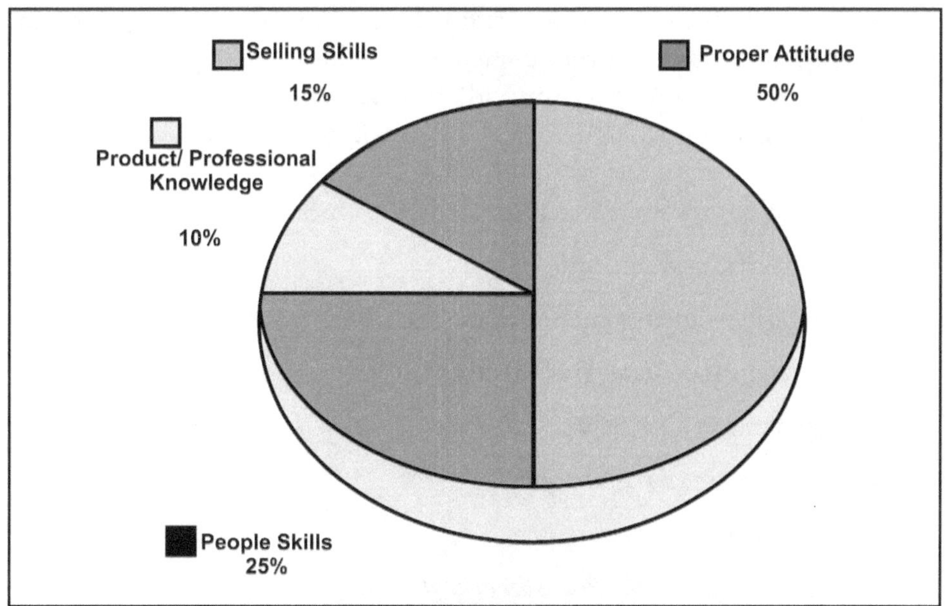

Illustration: Mental make-up of a Professional

As you will see, 50% has to do with the Attitude, followed by 25% on People Skills. In other words, if you don't have the required knowledge or skills to sell, as you can see, you may be able to still succeed with the right attitude and people skills, because those two account for 75%. Now don't get me wrong, I am not saying that you should not work on your knowledge and skills... Absolutely no!

What I am saying is that given that you have the right attitude coupled with the right people skills, knowledge and selling skills, you don't have to guess where your sales would be!

Let us look at this a little differently....Assuming you have the right attitude and people skills, which together comprise of 75% but lack the required knowledge and skills, well then, to me with the right attitude you can easily learn them. In any case Knowledge and Selling Skills are teachable, but not Attitude!

Attitude is the outlook or perception towards a given situation, and for a sales person this is crucial and foundational! Attitude is made up from our upbringing, environment, exposure etc. It would therefore be extremely difficult or it would take a long time to undo a wrong attitude that has gone in all these years. And for a Sales Person this is very important- as customers remember the wrong or negative attitude longer. You are the only thing the customer sometimes sees of your company- and this is the impression formed of your entire company- good or bad! It a takes a long time to undo this negative feeling about your company in the mind of the customer.

At this stage it is important to realize that there are **3 A's** of **Business life:**

Ability, Ambition and Attitude.

Ability establishes *'what'* someone does

Ambition determines *'how much'* he does

Attitude *'guarantees how'* he does it!

Ability will bring one a pay cheque

Ambition will get him a raise

Attitude alone will lead to success in everything!

Attitude is actually the 'YOU on the job. When ability and ambition in two people are about equal, how does the boss select one over the other for promotion? Here is where Attitude is the deciding factor. Attitude reflects a little plus- that something extra is given willingly though not required.

If you look at the word A-T-T-I-T-U-D-E itself, is it a mere coincidence that "I" comes first and "U" later? If this has any significance, then in trying to understand the attitudes of people, we should first examine ourselves in relation to other people!

Because Attitude is so very important, this is why it is so crucial to fill our minds with the right positive thoughts because our thoughts work into decisions that form our actions and this continued action leads to a habit, which eventually makes up our attitude. Your habits today will become your attitude in the days to come. That's why it is important to check our habits as well. As an example: The habit of late-coming, if not nipped in the early stages can lead it to becoming an attitude, with everything that you undertake being late or delayed!

Here are some examples of positive or right attitude:

Belief

Commitment

Desire

Ability to fail

Persistent goals

Self-Motivation

Enthusiasm

Purpose

Self-discipline

Confidence

Creativity

Empathy

Go the extra mile

Self-improvement

Time organization

...and most of all the *PASSION!*

Successful Sales People...

-Understand themselves and how their behavior affects their customers

-Have a positive attitude, which reflects in dedication to getting it right the first time, and commitment to help colleagues to help their customers

-Know how to adapt their behavior to meet the differing needs of the situation

-A willingness to take responsibility

-Have the confidence to stay calm under pressure

In studies conducted on what makes only a few stand apart as TOP performers, whilst the rest are mediocre, the following was seen as the difference:

Top Performer	Average Performer
- Plans Questions	- Plans Presentations
- Focuses on large strategic sales	- Focuses on quick hits
- Uses different strategies for different competitors	- Uses one strategy to cover all
- Gets quickly to business	- Spends a lot of time in Preliminary talk
- Asks question with impact	- Asks questions that have less focus and often seem to go nowhere
- Holds back from giving product details early in the sale	- Jumps in early in the sale with product presentations / description
- Doesn't talk about capabilities unless they are important to the customer	- Dumps product features and capabilities on the customer
- Ends the call by agreeing on next steps and joint action plans	- Often ends calls with no actions agreed

Steps to change your Attitude …

-Become aware of your negative attitude towards yourself, other people and situations and alter your thinking

-Think for yourself and become more constructive

-Keep an open mind

Remember: Changes are always: M.A.D.E...!!!

Developing Sales Attitudes is not something that happens to you-it is something you make happen...and like any change, it is not easy!

M- Mental Pictures: Visualize who you are, what you want, how will you conduct and carry yourself

A- Affirmations: Add a new self-image by talking positively

D- Daily Successes: Build confidence everyday by looking at your positives rather than negatives

E- Environmental Influences: Surround yourself with positive influencers, read positive stuff, listen and watch positive information etc

You are what you think! To change any habits, you must first change any thoughts, feelings and values!

Changing Bad Habits into Good Ones!

STEP # 1: List your bad habits

STEP # 2: What were the original causes?

STEP # 3: What are the supporting causes?

STEP # 4: Determine a positive habit to replace the bad one.

STEP # 5: Think about the good habit, its benefits and results.

STEP # 6: Take action to develop this habit.

STEP # 7: Daily act upon this habit for reinforcement.

STEP # 8: Reward yourself by noting one of the benefits from your good habit

EXERCISE

List some of the Key **Attitudes, Skills** and **Habits** that you possess?

1.

2.

3.

4.

5.

6.

7.

8.

9.

10

List some of the **Attitudes, Skills & Habits** that you lack or are weak in and need to work on?

1.

2.

3.

4.

5.

By When and What will you do specifically to improve or change the negatives to positives?

Action Plan

1.

2.

3.

4.

5.

SELL YOURSELF BEFORE YOU SELL ANYTHING ELSE!

A very important part that we would be touching on now is that of how we communicate or the impressions we create even before we could open our mouths.

In a study carried out that I am about to share with you now, you will notice that people place more emphasis on what they SEE rather than on what they HEAR.

So this only tells us that we need to be very careful with our body language and what we are projecting.

According to studies carried out, Communication takes place in 3 forms:

Your Words

Your Tone and

Your Body Language.

Where 55% has to do with your BODY LANGUAGE or what others SEE

7 % has to do with WHAT you say or your words

Whilst 38% has to do with HOW those words are said, which is your Tone or voice modulation

With people going by what they SEE first rather than what they HEAR, it makes it very important for us to therefore project the RIGHT image upfront. That's the impression that has been formed-good or bad! If it is good, then very good for you, but if it is bad, then so sad! Because…now you have double work to undo the wrong impression that has already gone into the mind and to now fill it with the right impression.

They say 90% of lasting impressions are created in the first 90 seconds. That can be really dangerous, but surprisingly that is true! So we have to be very careful, with what are we projecting as soon as someone sees us, because that's what they will remember.

It is also a reason why we tend to remember a song seen on a television set better than when heard through a radio. The same logic applies at a job interview with your resume and the presentation of it! Then at the interview-the interviewer has made up his mind to a great extent as you walk in, even before you have opened your mouth. Your bio-profile or the interview process is only a confirmation of the decision already made in the mind of the interviewer.

Why is Tone next important after Body Language? Simply because you can say a same sentence with a different tone and that can change the entire meaning

Eg; *"Mary come here"* is a simple sentence. But depending on the right tone this one sentence could turn out as an 'order 'or a 'request'.

Another stronger example: *"Hang him not let him go"*...could be death or life depending on how it is said. Example: *'Hang him, not let him go'!* Or *'Hang him not, let him go'!*

Now, if it is face to face, we may be able to save the situation, but when on the phone with the other person not able to see you, it could lead to miscommunication if the right tone is not used.

So as seen, with people going by what they SEE first rather than what they HEAR, it makes it so very important for us to therefore project the RIGHT image upfront. It basically involves Selling Yourself first!

Before a Customer buys anything or decides to do business with you or the company that you represent, he needs to first be sold on you because you are what he sees about your company to him. Your company could have a several floor building, with several offices all across the globe. But to the customer what he sees in you, is the impression he has formed of your company! Because...90% of lasting impressions are created in the first 90 seconds

So what could you do to improve your image- starting right from the top of your head to the tip of your toes- your hygiene, dressing and grooming, being organized etc. Given below is a suggested checklist to help you project the Right Image!

Checklist- Projecting the Right Image!

Mental- Your mind focused on the customer and not other issues

Physical Aspects like:

- ✓ Personal Grooming-Dress for the next level!
- ✓ Cleanliness, Breath (floss/ use mouthwash), Hair well groomed, Nails, Body Odour (light deodorant)
- ✓ Clean, Pressed/ Proper fit clothes

- ✓ Check for stains/ loose buttons
- ✓ Pleasant Colours of Clothing
- ✓ Polished shoes and in good condition (don't let heels run down)
- ✓ Socks (clean without holes, foot deodorant?)
- ✓ Clean Spectacles
- ✓ Briefcase/ handbag well polished/ in good condition
- ✓ Business Cards in pristine, crisp condition (in a holder)
- ✓ Good quality pens that write!
- ✓ Standing- shoulder square/ sitting- erect
- ✓ Sales Kit-Bag-organized /in order/ tidy
- ✓ Being Punctual/ Seeking Permission etc
- ✓ Mobile phones in silent or off

<u>EXERCISE</u>

Develop your own checklist now to suit your specific country and need.

(You might like to add on to the list above)

1.

2.

3.

4.

5.

6.

7.

8.

9.

10.

Hand-shakes and Business Cards

As part of your 1st impressions that you are going to create, is also your handshake and the presentation of your business card.

Let us look at the business cards first....

When presenting business cards, they must always be presented face up with the front portion of the card facing towards the customer, and if presenting with one hand as in most western countries then it must be held by the tip not covering any part of the text on the card.

Some Asian countries present cards with both hands. Whatever be the culture, please ensure the cards are never kept in a wallet as they would tend to get folded or bent at the edges or corner. All cards must be in pristine condition, crisp with no folds, wrinkles or soggy edges.

Whenever presenting the card, make eye contact, with a pleasant smile.

Handshakes...

While it is good to give the other person a firm handshake, it is also important to note that 'firm' should not mean 'bone-crushing' but just comfortable enough for the other person. In other words your handshake should convey 'CARE'!

(Think of: **CAIR- C**onfidence, **A**ssurance, **I**nterest, **R**espect)

That is why we recommend that you practice the exact firmness of your handshake first with your own hand. This could be done by taking your left hand out- 4 fingers together and thumb up with the hand facing inwards towards you, as if it is a customers' hand. Now take your right hand the usual way you would use to shake someone's hand and assuming that your left hand is your customers' hand, shake as follows: Web into web first followed by the 4 fingers of your right hand around your left hand, with the thumb finally locking. Basically 3 locks...web into web, 4 fingers around and thumbs interlocked. Since it is your own hand, you will know what amount of firmness to use.

Keep practicing till you are comfortable with the right amount of firmness to clasp the other person's hand without it being 'bone-crushing' or the opposite- too limp (a dead fish hand shake!)

You can do this exercise whenever you are free, till you get accustomed to the exact amount of pressure to be used.

WHY YOUR SELF-ESTEEM MATTERS! HOW TO BUILD A HIGH SELF ESTEEM

Confidence versus Self-Esteem

A lot has been said and published with a great debate on the subject of 'Confidence'. A lot of Sales people want to be more confident, without knowing the actual meaning of it.

A few points to note about confidence is that; it is 'External' and it is 'Temporary'. When I say external- I mean that in most times it is <u>not</u> in your Control- somebody else is most of the time controlling it. When I say it is temporary I believe that for a day our confidence levels fluctuate several times depending on situations, circumstances, the people and environment we are in. That is why we do not recommend that Sales People aim at only Confidence.

Here is an example of what I mean:

You come into the office in the morning in a good mood-upbeat and all excited with a set of appointments you have for the day. However, your boss calls you into his cabin and pulls you up for a complaint that has come in from a top customer. What happens to your confidence level...One that was upbeat, is now down depending on how hard he came upon you!

Later, that same evening, you have bagged a huge order from another customer and that same boss now praises you as one of his best performers. What happens now? You are on top of the world, all up beat and charged up again.

As you can see in a single day your confidence levels can vary and fluctuate, which means they are temporary. Most times it is the effect or impact of others that have changed that feeling. It is like someone having a remote control on your life and your moods that can change or impact it every now and then.

A better, permanent solution to this is for you as a Sales Person to work on having a High Self Esteem. First let us look at what is Self Esteem?

Simply put...It is how much you value or respect yourself! The more you value or respect yourself, then, when you do face such situations like the example we've just seen, you are able to stay above- your value if it is 100, stays 100 and does not change! You now know that your boss has pulled you up for something wrong that you had done- but that does not change your value- it still remains 100.

Building your Self Esteem

Say out loud:
"I am the Most Valuable Person at work".
"I am the Most Valuable Person at my work". (Repeat it)

It's true. You are the most valuable person. No one else can quite fill your shoes. No one else can be you. You bring your unique being to work every day. You bring with you your talents, your abilities, your knowledge, your skills, your personality, or just your plain know-how. You may not be using all of your abilities just yet. You may not be using them to the fullest. You may not even recognize how valuable a person you are.

Healthy Self Esteem, not narcissistic, self-indulgent, or arrogance means to appreciate the value of you as a unique human being with your own special talents and abilities.

The word "esteem" in Latin, means, *"to value highly"*

It would be impossible to value another person without first feeling valuable for yourself. When you place value on your own work and efforts, you can begin to find value in the work of others.

The Self-Image: Highway to Success

Have you ever said to yourself the following?
'I can't imagine myself being successful'
'I would like to, but I don't have enough experience or the right education'
'I can't get ahead because I'm too short, overweight, not good looking, my parents are poor, etc'.
The truth is most people talk themselves into failure and dejection. The result is the Fear of Trying.

Most of us know of or have read about common, everyday people who have become uncommonly productive and successful in their work and careers; individuals who have overcome enormous outer obstacles and inner roadblocks to become great.

Yet many people can't imagine doing such things themselves. They say, "*Yes, he could do it or she's doing it, but I can't because of*______________".

They develop the habit of failure. And it takes two forms:

Failure Reinforcement-the habit of looking back at past problems
Failure Forecasting-the habit of imagining the worst in the future

Because they lack sufficient self-esteem to believe in the validity of their dreams, they don't prepare for their achievement, and therefore are going down a dead-end street.

No wonder so many people feel trapped. Failure becomes set in their self-images.

Never put yourself down- the workplace is full of put-downs- Don't do it yourself!

Self Esteem Takes Practice

Believe in yourself, no matter how long it takes or how tough it may seem at times.

There was once a college professor whose wife had a hearing deficiency. In trying to invent a device to enhance her hearing, he created something more complex that he thought might be useful to the public. He traveled throughout the New England states trying to find venture capital to take his idea into production. But businessmen everywhere laughed at him. *"Ideas are a dime a dozen."* They said: *"The project is doomed to failure."* Thank goodness, Alexander Graham Bell had the self-esteem to hang in there even when his only reward was his belief in himself.

Often we put imaginary barriers in our paths when no such barriers actually exist. In the 1940s, the greatest physicist and aeronautical engineers believed that the sound barriers could not be broken- that everyone or anything would be shattered when it approached the speed of sound. One lone pilot, Chuck Yeager, didn't believe it. He didn't think there was such a thing as sound "barrier". And indeed, he flew right through it.

Your Formula for Building a High Self-Esteem

How much you like yourself is the core energy force that determines your personality.

All top performers have a program or formula for building self-esteem.

Steps You Can Take To Feel Better:

1. Action precedes feeling. Act your way into feeling something. Action triggers emotion. The role of pretending- act happy!
2. Set clear goals, so you can feel like a winner. Establish a VICTORY

LIST for all your accomplishments. Set income goals (the WHAT) and personal goals (the WHY)

3. Accept 100% responsibility. "IF IT'S TO BE, IT'S UP TO ME." Or "IF IT'S ALL FOR ME, IT'S UP TO ME". No excuses, no blaming.

4. Commit yourself to excellence. LEARN TO BE THE BEST in whatever you do. Say to yourself: *'I'M THE BEST (and) I LOVE MY WORK'*

5. Mental Rehearsal: Visualize the outcomes you desire, especially before you go to sleep at night. See yourself as strong, confident and relaxed, and see your customers responding positively.

6. Get yourself a small note pad. Every night write down at least 3 positive things you did for that day- (it could be as small as even helping a person cross the road). Forget the negatives. Most times we go to bed filling our minds with all the negatives that occurred during the day. Just reverse it now. Look at only the positives. At the end of the year, you would have over one thousand positive things about you. Do you need any else then to tell you?

7. Believe in yourself-FAITH! Believe in yourself, your company and your products.

8. INTEGRITY AND HONESTY. They are at the root of success in sales. Never expect to be successful without being willing to pay the price. Never expect the rewards without working. Don't look for shortcuts.

9. Have confident expectations. Look for the good in every situation. Expect the best.

10. Practice the Law of Increasing Returns-the more your give thanks, the more you will have thanks for.

KEY ACTIVITIES OF A PROFESSIONAL CONSULTATIVE SALES PERSON
(EFFECTIVELY MANAGING YOUR DAY AND ACTIVITIES)

In this chapter, we would be looking at how a Sales Person works a typical day by managing his activities and how he could get the most out of it

What you will notice below is an example of 'A Poor Sales Person' versus 'A Successful Person'. Notice the difference in time spent on each activity?

Poor Sales Person	
Prospecting	10%
Sales Presentation	23%
Service	15%
Administration	30%
Travel	20%
Self-improvement	2%

Successful Sales Person	
Prospecting	55%
Sales Presentation	10%
Service	20%
Administration	5%
Travel	10%
Self-improvement	10%

The Successful Sales Person knows the importance of prospecting. That's the pipeline for future business or rather your company's insurance to a better tomorrow. So his majority of time is spent in this area.

With proper planning, by identifying and fixing appointments with the right decision maker, the Successful Sales Person is able to effectively and productively work on only the right ones, thus, not wasting precious time.

Now notice anything on the total of the percentages in both the scenarios? While the Poor Sales Persons' total is100, the Successful Sales Persons total is110!!

How is this possible? How is the Successful Sales Person able to do 10% more activities, besides being more productive too, in the same number of hours given to both?

As an example, you see the Successful Salesperson does not waste precious time when waiting to meet prospects. He effectively uses that time, reading or developing himself or fixing appointments for the next day or week or even preparing his reports. These are a few examples of him using his time effectively. Thus the Successful Sales Person is able to accomplish more activities in the same time compared to the Poor Sales Person, whilst yet being very successful

How could YOU get more productive with the same number of hours given to everyone equally?

Let us look at a typical day in the life of a Sales Person. Here is an example.

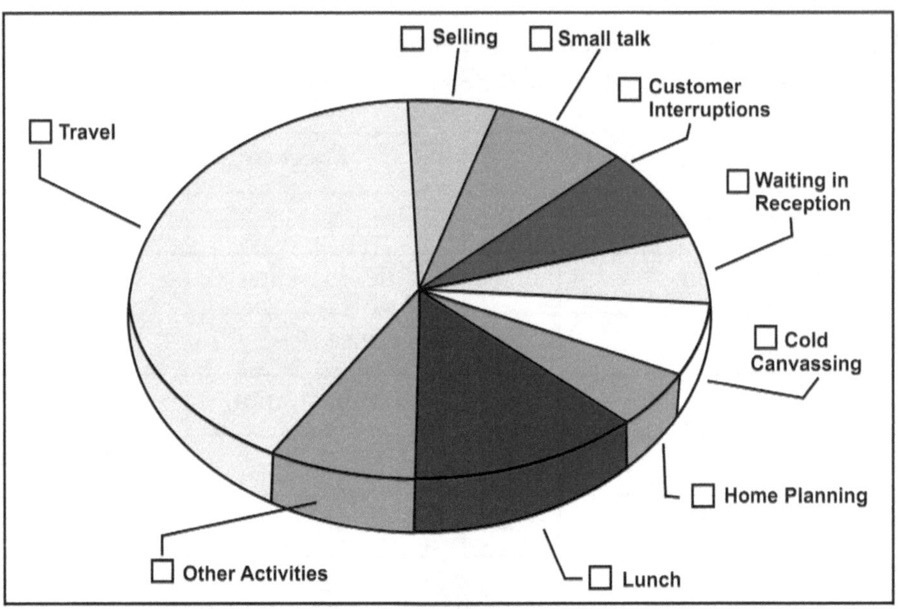

Illustration: An example of a day in the life of a Sales person

If you look at the pie chart on the screen, you will see a typical scenario of a sales person's average day. This was taken from surveys of several field sales personnel's typical days activities.

As can be seen only 8 to 10% of the sales person's time is actually spent on his core function which is selling! Now just imagine this: If this person who is spending 8 to 10% of this time and brings in 100% quota, what would happen if that 8 to 10% is marginally increased to let's say 15 to 20%? What do you think would happen to his productivity? Obviously double!

Now, it may not be possible to eliminate all that unnecessary stuff seen in that pie-chart above, but I'm sure if that same sales person is to work his day smarter, he would be able to get more out of it. As you will learn it is all about planning your day, focusing and prioritizing on the right activities at the right time.

Let us see how?

Every Sales Person, I believe has only **4 Key Activities** for a day irrespective of whatever you sell, and all what you do...it could be a 100 different things, but they broadly can be classified or covered under these 4 key headings:

Planning
Prospecting
Selling
Administration

If you had to rate these 4 activities in an order of importance- what do you think would rank as number 1, 2, 3 and 4 respectively? Have a try before you see the recommended answer that follows!

The most important activities for any Sales Person, and to put across a little stronger-is what he or she is paid to do- **Prospecting** and **Selling**. If you are spending anything lesser than 75% on these 2 areas then you would need to look at revamping your working schedule. These 2 Activities are the only ones that account for being revenue generators. The other 2 are only support functions.

Planning is the scheduling of your activities- long, medium and short term, while also including your meetings with bosses, other departments etc.

Some examples of Planning are:

Planning next week's calendar

Working on an annual or monthly sales plan

Planning the day's calls

Meeting with manager to discuss targets and results

Researching potential customers

Analysing the existing client base

Administration is the time you spend on the preparation of your reports, documentation, market feedback, travel expenses etc.

Some examples are:
Preparing reports
Updating customer records/ CRM
Preparing Travel bills
Attending training courses
Travelling to appointments

Prospecting involves time spent in sourcing new potential opportunities and the bulk of your time should go here, because this is your insurance to future business. This is like a pipeline to continuous business.

Some examples are:
Tele-calling potential customers
Requesting for referrals
Visiting/ Scouting the market
Attending Exhibitions and Fairs
Cold canvassing

Selling is the actual time you spend on phone or in person with a customer.

Some examples are:
Fixing Appointments
Fact finding to uncover needs
Presentation in front of customers
Follow up visit for decision
Telephone call for decision
Negotiating terms and conditions

Unfortunately, many sales people fall into what is called the *'Activity Trap',* where they measure their effectiveness by how *hard* they work, rather than by how *smart* they work.

A good time to schedule your Planning and Administration Activities would be during the non peak business hours or when your customers are not usually available, as the peak of business hours should be for Prospecting and Selling, when you should be there with the customer. If you are not, remember, your competition will be there!

Now try breaking your entire days' activities under these 4 heads, and look at scheduling your non sales Activities during the lean times.

EXERCISE

Break your day into 4 key areas, listing Activities and Time:

	Activities	Time
Planning:		
1.		
2.		
3.		

4.

5.

6.

7.

8.

Prospecting:

1.

2.

3.

4.

5.

6.

7.

8.

Selling:

1.

2.

3.

4.

5.

6.

7.

8.

Administration:

1.

2.

3.

4.

5.

6.

7.

8.

Daily Call Monitoring

As a Sales Professional, it is important in your own interest to keep a track of all your calls and the outcome.

Here is an example of a 'Contact Activity Log' that you could use every day. You could have this set into your desktop or laptop or even on your mobile, thus helping you be more organized.

CONTACT ACTIVITY LOG

Sales Professional				Date		
Company	Contact	Type of Call	Rating (A, B, C)	Remarks - Outcome	Time In	Time Out

Type of Call	PA - Phone Appointment	P - Presentation	V - Appointment (Visit)
I - Incoming Call	S - Status / Follow - up	CC - Cold Call	NI - Not Interested

Illustration: Daily Call Monitoring: 'Contact Activity Log'

When planning your Day, it is a good idea to have a 'M.A.P.':

M ake a **daily 'To Do'** list of Key Activities
A ction   A Important AND Urgent ('must')
            B Important NOT Urgent ('should')
            C Urgent not Important ('could')
P rioritise A – B – C order daily

THE SELLING PROCESS- THE 6 STEP SELLING PLAN OUTLINE

Only now we are actually getting into the Selling Process...so before we go any further, let us ask ourselves: What is Selling? What comes to your mind when you hear the word 'Selling' or 'Sale'?

I can guarantee you that for most sales people, the very first words that pop up in our minds would be words like *'revenue, profits, quotas, targets, etc'...* all related to money! Shouldn't this then only confirm what came up in the survey (that we seen earlier) on 'What customers hate about Sales People'? We are more concerned with what is in the customers' wallet, his checkbook or the order, than genuinely helping the customer.

But if we could change that thinking to a feeling that Selling is more of *'Problem Solving'*, it would then change our entire perspective of the Selling process and the way we treat the customer particularly. Let us now change that hat that we have been wearing from a Sales Person to that of a Consultant or Advisor! Someone has a problem and our job is to genuinely help that person get out of that problem or situation, then only will our whole perception towards the selling process change.

It is like what happens when a patient visits a doctor. A genuine doctor, will never prescribe, until he has really diagnosed the problem completely. When this happens the customers' confidence and respect for the sales person zooms up. He now begins to trust you as the sales person, thus leading to rapport and a lasting relationship

If you look at the word 'SALE' – the word actually tells you in an acronym the steps that one should follow.

Most times, a sales person, just rushes into providing his pitch on the product or service that he represents, without actually taking time to understand the need of a customer. This acronym should be a reminder for us to

<u>S</u>TOP (think!)

<u>A</u>sk Questions (to understand the need of the customer),

<u>L</u>isten to understand...and finally

<u>E</u>ngage, Enthuse & Excite the customer, by letting the customer do more of the talking

The Foundation of the Sales Process

What do you think could be the reason that makes someone buy from a Particular Company or Salesperson?

You will be surprised to note that most times, the reason is neither the product, nor the price, but rather the **relationship** with the person with whom they're dealing.

Products will change, services will change, prices will change, economies and market places will change too– but if the relationship is strong, the account endures.

I have seen many accounts move as the sales person moved from the company too.

The only thing that truly matters is the <u>relationship</u> between the seller and the buyer.

When you don't have an edge in product technology or price, then you need an edge in the way you <u>connect</u> with people.

The foundation of Relationship is an important word: TRUST. To make a buying decision, a customer has to make a leap of faith. Successful salespeople create a safety net called trust. Trust helps your customers take that leap in complete confidence.

This is what Relationship or Consultative Selling can do. Unlike the Hard Sell Approach, in relationship or collaborative selling, the salesperson takes time up front to build a sincere, committed relationship by investing time in learning about the customer's needs. Then, every step of the sales process that follows is conducted with the relationship in mind. This ensures an enduring and lasting relationship, leading to repeat business and referrals

<u>The 6 Step Selling Cycle</u>

From this module, we would be entering into the Selling Cycle comprising of 6 steps:

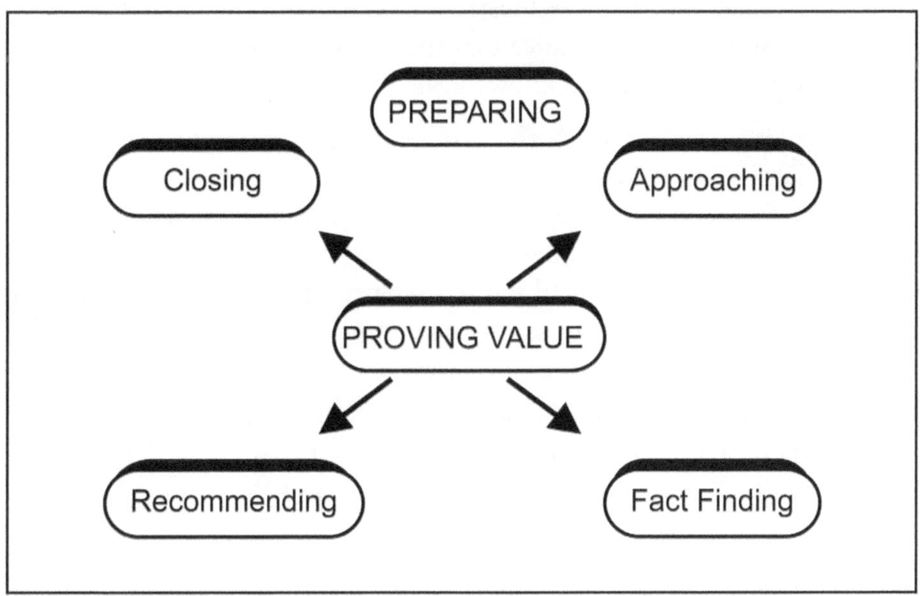

Illustration: The 6 Step Selling Plan: At-a-glance

You will notice in the illustration that there are 6 steps to Professional Selling-at a glance. If you were asked to pick the 3 most important steps according to you, what do you think they would be? Go ahead have a guess, before I provide what I believe are the 3 'most-important-never-to-skip' steps! (What comes up from you?)

Here are the 3 'most-important-never-to-skip' steps!

1. Preparation

2. Fact-finding

3. Proving Value

But distressingly, a good majority of the 'so called sales people' out there totally skip these three steps and move into the other three steps of Approaching, Recommending and Closing. They greet the customer, and then believe they know or assume his need (as the sales lead could have been through an enquiry or referral) and so now because of the mismatch of the customers' real need and the sales persons assumed need, there is now a struggle to close.

This could be a total 'put-off' for the customer. The sales person has no right to recommend, without uncovering the customers' exact need or problem.

From the 6 Step Selling Cycle illustration, you will notice that there are 2 interesting points...Did you notice that the step of Preparing is isolated from the other 5 steps...And do you know why?

For two major reasons: Because this is done before meeting the client-usually at your office and the other reason is that, this is the step that can set the tone for a positive outcome. You have no right to a customer's time if you aren't prepared. If you want someone to have confidence and invest several dollars with you in business, then in all fairness we need to do some work upfront. This also helps you stand out from the competition. ..The Customer feels confident dealing with someone who cares!

The other interesting point that stands out is the fact that Proving Value is placed right in the centre of the others...Reason being...Everything you say revolves or centers on the perceived value of your product or service in the eyes of the customer

The average Sales Person out there usually spends less time in trying to understand the need of the customer, and because of which ends on a mismatch when providing the solution. It's a solution that may not usually match the need and hence the sales person always has objections that he has to encounter and because of which may eventually lose a sale together with credibility!

However, with the Consultative Approach the sales person spends a lot of time up front in trying to unravel the specific need of the customer. When this happens there is now a clear match with the solution provided. It leads to both the customer and sales person working as partners, building trust along, where the customer is involved in the solution, thus bringing down the objections that the traditional sales person faces.

PREPARING AND PLANNING YOUR CALL

<u>The First Step- Preparation</u>

The first step in the Consultative Selling Skills Cycle is **Preparation.**

As preparation is the first step in the selling plan, it can as such, be likened to the foundation of the call. **Preparation is vital, as it provides the research required to pursue an intelligent and productive interview.**

Before we go any further into this, let us first ask: Why Prepare?

- ✓ *Makes you feel more confident*
- ✓ *You are able to discuss intelligently*
- ✓ *Saves time – yours & customer*
- ✓ *Get to understand customer potential needs*
- ✓ *Become more aware of business*
- ✓ *Prepare a good recommendation*
- ✓ *Study competition*
- ✓ *Your customers respect for you goes up*
- ✓ *Professional in the eyes of the customer*
- ✓ *Customer knows you are there to help- not extract*

A Sales person has no right to call or visit a customer if he hasn't prepared for the account.

On the other hand, when a customer sees a Sales Person as being prepared, his respect for the sales person and the company that he represents zooms up.

How fair is it to a customer when a sales person tries to solicit business that is worth several thousands or millions of money, without doing any groundwork for the customer? When a customer is going to part with several thousands of his money, shouldn't you as a Sales person do some amount of ground work before meeting or contacting him. This is what will lead to respect, resulting in enhanced credibility and a lifelong relationship, because now the customer can see clearly that you, as the sales person are genuinely interested in helping him, and not just after his money!

A lot of people think that Selling has a lot to do with 'being lucky'!

My answer is that Good Selling is not a 'matter of Luck', but rather a combination of Preparation plus Opportunity where Preparation accounts for 99%. Now when 99% of efforts have been put in, and that 1% opportunity gets by you, then that is what will make you the so called 'lucky person'

But if you are unprepared and that 1% opportunity comes by, it will just go past you and move to someone more prepared. That is why preparation is the key to a successful sale.

I call it being an 'Eagle System Seller' and just as how an Eagle is focused and watchful, an Eagle System Seller spends more than 55% on this step alone, as he prefers to 'prepare than repair' or have any regrets later.

Analyzing Accounts

Before you start to prepare on an individual account, you would need to analyze the different accounts assigned to you or in your territory so this could help you prioritize your sales calls.

In the 1st illustration below, you could list your accounts in the boxes that best correspond to the combinations of '**Sales Volume**' and '**Profits**'. Your goal should be to work your accounts so they move up in 'Sales Volume' and 'Profitability'.

ANALYZE YOUR ACCOUNTS

SALES VOLUME

	Low	Medium	High
High			
Medium			
Low			

(PROFITABILITY)

The next step would be to classify your accounts in terms of 'Profitability' and prioritizing them to determine how and when to call on them. Using the 2nd illustration below, you could use the data from your past (last one year) and rank your accounts by their profitability. You could do this separately for each product line or service.

ANALYZE YOUR ACCOUNTS

	Company	Contact	Phone
"A" Accounts Top 20% Very Profitable			
"B" Accounts Middle 30% Profitable			
"C" Accounts Bottom 50% Less Profitable			
PROSPECTS			

Illustration: Analyzing your Accounts

Preparing for Individual Accounts

The step of Preparation for an individual account, involves compiling and analyzing relevant client information and developing an appropriate sales call strategy on how to handle the customer

The Purpose of Preparing is to have an overview of the client's current status with your company (as a new or existing customer), the competition, the industry and marketplace which will allow you to approach him in an appropriate way.

Being the first and key part in the Consultative Selling Cycle, it consists of **5 key steps:**

The **1st step** is all about preparing yourself-the mental and physical self, which we have already covered in an earlier module

The **2nd Step** is preparing information related to the customer...things like, who is the contact person or decision maker, who are they currently dealing with and for how long, how happy are they with this set up, how do they pay. These are just a few thoughts. You could build your own checklist in the Exercise that follows.

The 3rd Step is all about the Market, the Industry and the Competition.... Examples would be: What is the market like, who are the other players, where does your organization stand in relation or comparison with them. What are their USP's etc? How does your company or products compare with the competition- the strengths/ weaknesses etc? The more details you have, you will be in a better position when meeting the customer.

The 4th Step is...what you need to carry or take with you on this call that can help you...things like your business cards, pens that write, note pad, a power point presentation, your brochures, pricelists, testimonials etc.

And finally the **5th Step** is your Call Strategy...How are you planning on making this first contact- your approach, what are you going to say, what are the questions you are planning to ask to uncover the customers' need , what are the type of concerns you could expect and how would you go about handling them.

Basically this 5th step is more of a role play of the entire call in your mind before meeting the customer that would set you up for success. Obviously you will be more confident with doing this 5th step only after you have covered all steps of this 6 step selling plan

Depending on the market you are in and the customer, selling on Credit could be a very important decision. If your company's policy is to sell on credit in your market, then one of the key areas you'd like to keep in mind before you get the customer into your fold is to assess his creditworthiness or his ability to pay you...and on time!

Now this takes several checks...and given below are some suggestions to help you.

- *Past Records.*
- *Sales Representatives Reports (In House Opinion)*
- *Bank Reference.*
- *Trade Associations.t*
- *Chambers Of Commerce.*
- *Credit Rating Agencies.*
- *Visit to Customers Premise.*

- *Market Feedback.*
- *Press Reports.*
- *Directorate of Foreign Trade*
- *Registrar Of Companies (Annual Reports)*
- *Customers Suppliers/ Service Providers*
- *Stock Exchange Opinion.*
- *Life of Business.*
- *Nature f Business.*
- *Reference Checks*
- *Family Background*
- *Assets*
- *Website*

You don't have to check into all of these areas, but a good indicative way or thumb rule would be if you find 4 to 5 areas positive, it should tell you that the road is fairly clear to move ahead...but if you do have a few red areas, then you will need to do further probing or investigation on the customers standing in the market.

Remember: As sales people the temptation is always for more business without having to carry out such checks. However, prevention is better than cure! One rotten apple can mess your entire basket soon...Word travels fast! So treat this step with caution.

Another checklist you as a Sales Person would like to build up on is the items in your kit or brief case. A suggested sample list is what you see below...however start building your own.

- *Business Cards*
- *Diary/ Note Pad*
- *Pens that write*
- *Visual aids/Brochures*
- *Testimonials*
- *Best Rates*
- *Competition Statistics*
- *News Articles*
- *Proposal*
- *PPT Presentation for larger corporates...etc*

Customers like to deal with organized people that do not waste their time. Also if the customer sees you as being organized, his respect for you will go up, while being assured that his business would also be handled in an orderly way! Nobody would want to deal with someone who is messy or disorganized.

<u>When preparing it is a good idea to:</u> Think of 4 Cs

Customer, Competitor, Capabilities, and Cost (Value)

Customer:

Do they know us? What information do they have about us?

Do we know them in any way? What information do we have about them?

Competitor:

-Who are the Competitors?

-What are their positions in the eyes of the customer?

-How does the customer see/ perceive them?

-Brainstorm their Strengths/Weaknesses

-Has an examination of your competitors' strengths or weaknesses uncovered sufficient reason to warrant re-examination of your initially selected strategy

-What aspects of the requirement which (from your knowledge of your competition) you can speculate your competitor will address more effectively than you.

-Is There any Impact on Your Selected Strategy? It is important that you re-examine your selected strategy again-in the light of your competitors' strengths and weaknesses.

-Is there anything there that weakens your case sufficiently for you to consider a change of strategy?

Capabilities:

What are our capabilities?

Do we stand out from the competition? In what areas?

Cost (Value)

What value are we bringing to the customer? How would he view it?

Preparing for Existing Customers!

When preparing for existing customers, you might like to keep the following in mind:

- *Analyze any Weaknesses in Your Solution*
- *Are there any show-stoppers?*
- *Are there any points that will render the selected strategy ineffective? If so, then reconsider your decision on strategy*

Study Past Successes- Some Generic Strategies

Cost

You might well have won the business for one of the following reasons:

Lowest price, or Best price/performance, or (ROI).

Technical Aspects

In this instance the lead decision-maker was most likely a senior technical officer in the client organisation. You may have won because of: Superior specifications or program/ solution design, or better technical personnel.

Quality

A quality orientation can manifest itself in either of two ways: "Snob" value or proven high quality/reliability.

Competitiveness

There are 2 ways you may have found your proposals were successful:

The extent to which you proved that your solution was vastly superior to that of any of your competition, or the extent to which you convinced your client that your solution would afford them some significant competitive edge over their own competition.

Credibility

Whether the lead decision-maker was technically, financially or administratively oriented, the credibility of your organisation could have been a compelling argument for or against your proposal. You could have been selected because of: Who your organisation is or your team members or industry experience.

EXERCISE

Now try making your own Checklist before going to meet the customer:

A. Self- Mental/ Physical

1.

2.

3.

4.

5.

6.

7.

8.

9.

10.

B. Client Info: (including Creditworthiness)

1.

2.

3.

4.

5.

6.

7.

8.

9.

10.

C. Market/ Industry/ Competition Information:

1.

2.

3.

4.

5.

6.

7.

8.

9.

10.

D. Sales Tools:

1.

2.

3.

4.

5.

6.

7.

8.

9.

10.

Note, that we are not doing an exercise on the 5th Step which is 'Call Strategy' as this can be done only after you know or have covered all the other steps of the sales process.

So as can be seen, for you to be an effective Sales Person you will need to work on being organized and have **SYSTEM.S.** When you do have **SYSTEMS**, you will find that it will help...

Save

You

Stress

Time

Energy

Money and...

Sleepless Nights!

While also enhancing your credibility & productivity!

At this stage of the Sales Cycle, it is important as Sales Professionals to try and understand the mind of the buyer

The key Rule is to always try to find out where or at which phase of the buying process the client is currently in:

If in phase 1- then we are First-Great!

Good to be No.1, as people tend to remember those first. (Example; If I asked you who was the 1st person to climb mount Everest or go to the moon- you would certainly know the answer. But very rarely or we may find it difficult remembering the 2nd or 3rd person that did so!)

If in phase 2- then we may <u>not</u> be First!

Let us look at Phase 1- if we are first. It is important for us to determine his needs and obviously there could be 4 stages to put across, in a simplified manner

1. They Need Something

2. Rough idea-What would it be/ look like?

3. Rough Cost- Affordability?

4. Finally...the Sources-Who can help them?

Now that the customer has the various sources in front of him, he enters Phase 2 wherein he begins to evaluate the options in front.

In other words what's best for his company and where can he avail the services from?

He now moves to Phase 3 which involves Evaluating of Risks in doing business with a new supplier. Right on top of his mind, would in most times be the Quality of Service followed by the Rate or Pricing.

A point to note is that price can never stand alone and is always related to quality. The next area that the client would probably evaluate is if your prices match his current budgets set for this. Here is where transparency is very important where he would like to have a clear break up of your working.

Lastly, the customer would like to consider the fact that should the vendor mess up at some stage, then how would the vendor handle such situations?

This is where having a good list of satisfied customers can help, with words like:

"If you don't believe me-Ask my clients!" (A third and independent opinion is always helpful and important)

APPROACHING CUSTOMERS
(PHONE AND FACE-TO-FACE)

The Second Step in the Consultative Selling Cycle is Approach

Approaching is the **second step** in the Consultative Selling Cycle and is the process of making your first or initial contact with a client. The initial customer contact is an important part of the interview as it "sets the tone" or establishes the climate for the rest of the interview.

Beginning the interview, the sales representative should anticipate a few potential customer deterrents to buy:

Apprehensions about the Salesperson

Apprehensions about the Company

Apprehensions about the Product

Buyer's Resistance

Price Concerns

At this stage, therefore, the sales person should be sensitive to the customer's apprehension about himself and his company.

So the purpose of the Approach step is to build rapport and provide an opportunity to move to the next step to uncover client needs ie; to help you to move to the next step in the Consultative Selling Cycle which is Fact Finding.

There are three types of approaches we could use in making initial contact with a client:

- The Telephone
- Face-to-face (Premise)
- or E-mail

Regardless of which approach is used, the initial contact should contain basically three vital elements:

- A reason for contacting the client
- An indication of the next step you plan to take
- A request for action

Since most of the time, the initial contact is made on phone; we'd like to particularly concentrate on the telephone approach. In terms of both the **content** (the words used) and the **style** (the way in which the content is delivered) an effective telephone approach consists of three parts:

- The Introduction
- The Body and the
- The Close

We have seen in an earlier module how Communication takes place with Words, Tone and Body Language. Now when it comes to communicating over the telephone, the most important percentage of 55% which comes from body language will be missing, with only 45% part being active with your Words and Tone. This means that our communication is only 45% effective if not done carefully. Therefore in order to compensate for this missing 55% we would need to work on our enthusiasm levels with our 'attitude' and 'voice modulation'.

The introduction must cover 5 key components:

The Salutation
Your Name
Your Company (that you represent)!
One line about what your company does- An attention grabber!
Check Convenient time
Your Purpose of Calling

You begin by wishing the customer, then identifying yourself first and then your company, followed by one key point on what your company does relevant to this customer's interest. (An important point to note here is to try and not use a *'Hi'* or *'Hello'* as a salutation- this sounds very unprofessional. A real professional approach would be a *'Good Morning, Afternoon or Evening'* as the case may be) Next check to see if you have called at a convenient time. If not, ask when it would be more convenient.

Explain the purpose of the call.

The Body is one of the trickiest parts, and is also referred to as using an ICR or Interest Creating Remark. In fact, this part can make your call stand out from the several other calls that your customer will be receiving for the day. And if you can master how to do this, you will be able to gain entries into most places. It is based on the principle that people like to hear or talk more about themselves than want to listen to others. Keeping this in mind, it is important to do a little bit of research earlier. Find out what is something new or exciting happening currently at the customers organization. It could be that they have bagged an Award, or you'd seen an article about their growth or expansion plans, or an article about their CEO. Something is always happening in every organization. We only need to be interested. Use this to congratulate or appreciate them. It can do wonders! This also gives them the feeling that you care about them and are aware of what is happening! Surprisingly, this helps them be more open now to what you've got to say!

Once you've got their attention, you now ask if it would be ok for you to ask a few questions in order to better understand their business, gradually moving them to the next step of the Selling Cycle.

A simple example would be as follows:

'Good Morning/ Afternoon' Mr. So & So (Sir or Mr, as the case may be, or whatever you are most comfortable with, though I recommend using the Customers name) 'This is 'Gerard' calling from Citius, Altius, Fortius Unlimited.

As you are probably aware, we are an over 18 year old leading international training company, with presence in 6 countries' specializing in providing training solutions to help your people grow, thus enabling your business soar!

Before I go any further Mr So & So, I'd like to check to see if I've called you at a convenient time (or you may like to also use... *'Is it a good time to talk to you?'*)

'The purpose in me calling you this (morning or afternoon as the case may be) *Mr. So and So, is to see how we could work along with you in providing a solution to some of your training and human resource challenges'.*

(Don't talk anything more-This becomes the 'Intro' part of your Approach)

The Body is one of the trickiest parts as explained earlier and if done well can help see you making an entry really easy. As an example you could say something like... *'Oh by the way, before I go any further, Congratulations on that new plant you've opened in Malaysia...We were so happy to read about this in the news! "*

Now this has to be done with a lot of enthusiasm and a genuine feeling of excitement. And the moment you say something that concerns them you've got their attention. Their usual reaction would be something like... *'Oh when or where did you see that news article? Can I get a copy?"* or *'Thanks a lot...yes we've got some new challenges ahead now"*

Whatever be their response, you've got their attention at this stage.

We now move to the 'Close' part of this step, by saying something like: *'In order for me to better understand your business, could I take a few minutes of your time to ask you a few questions that will help me better understand it.*

Also I'd like to take some notes as we go along...Is it ok with you?"

(This last line of asking to take notes- even though on phone and the customer can't see you do so, is vital! It subtly tells the customer that you are interested and you are there to help him. The competitor that called earlier did not do this- they were more on getting the business!)

<u>EXERCISE</u>

Using the structure explained above, work on your own script for the Approach Step.

Once you've written it, role-play it a few times in your mind, till you get the flow and gain confidence.

Introduction: (Cover the 5 points mentioned above)

____
____
____
____
____
____

Body: (The Interest creating remark!)

____
____
____
____
____
____

Close: (Permission to move to the next step: Fact-finding!)

____
____
____

What we just covered above is an example of approaching a new customer. But for existing customers you might prefer a different approach that could start off by building further...

1. **Rapport** (Start with something pleasant and interesting to the customer!) You could then get into your...

2. **Introduction:** By saying something like: *'Thank you for meeting me today...What I'd like to do in the next 30 minutes is...*

   a) Share information on our Company

   b) You and Your Situation

   c) Mutually see whether worthwhile continuing

Is that ok as an agenda for you?

(For particularly old clients you might like to share some new developments of your company)

And in case you are new to meeting this old client of your company, you might want to add *'...and I have been with* (name your company) *for the past ....'* (to build confidence)

Enough about me, now tell me about you and your situation

Now before we go deep into the third step of Fact-Finding, it is important that we invest some time in trying to see who the key decision makers are or what is the typical decision making process. **The earlier the better!** Studies show that sales people make several visits only to realize later that they wasted their precious time talking to the wrong people or to somebody that did not have the authority to take things forward.

You need to identify all those involved in the decision-making chain.

- *Who all are involved?*
- *Their Role- Purpose of their job*
- *Their Responsibility- What is the main function of job-holder*
- *Authority level- Who ultimately has the power to sign-off limits*

Key Points to Understanding the Decision Process

- *WHO? Who will decide on this Order/ Tender/ Bid/ Contract/ Award?*
- *WHAT? What is their decision making criteria?*
- *WHY? Why will they base their decision on that?*

- *WHEN? When will they be involved?*
- *WHERE? Where do they have influence?*
- *HOW? How can I positively influence them?*

You could use any of the following 3 acronyms to help you remember how to Qualify Customers?

W.A.N.T.S. Framework

- ✓ *Wants- Exactly what are they looking for?*
- ✓ *Authorities- Decision making process- What level of influence do they have on making decisions?*
- ✓ *Needs- Organisational goals- Does the Prospect have a Need worth Solving?*
- ✓ *Timescales- Evaluation and implementation- How soon they need a solution?*
- ✓ *Spend Capacity- Budget and when available- Do they have or can they find the ability to spend money on solving these challenges?*

The B.A.N.T. Framework

- ✓ *Budget: Is the prospect capable of buying?*
- ✓ *Authority: Does your contact have adequate authority to sign off on a purchase?*
- ✓ *Need: Does the prospect have a business pain you can solve?*
- ✓ *Timeline: When is the prospect planning to buy?*

The F.A.I.N.T. Framework

- ✓ *Funds- Money?*
- ✓ *Authority- Decision , Key Authority*
- ✓ *Interest, Eagerness, Desire*
- ✓ *Need, Pain area*
- ✓ *Timing, When?*

Now here's an **important tip** that top sales people use just before they could put down the phone after having obtained an appointment to take forward...

Always assign your prospect some Homework on Uncovering Pain Areas:

Give your prospect some homework before the appointment. You could begin by saying the following:

"Mr. Prospect, In order to make our meeting as productive as possible, would you make a list of the two or three most challenging issues you are having with respect to .....? Then we can really focus our discussion on these issues and try to develop a solution. Does that make sense?"

FACT-FINDING: UNCOVERING THE NEEDS AND PAINS OF CUSTOMERS

The Third and another very important step as mentioned earlier, is the 'Fact-finding' or 'Uncovering of Needs' Stage. This step and the next which is Proving Value can really make that big difference between you and the competition.

Fact Finding is the process of uncovering the client' needs, problems, opportunities or pain areas by which can be solved by the products or services of your company.

The purpose of Fact Finding is to obtain information that will allow you to move to the next step which is Proving Value

The extent to which Fact Finding is effectively completed will significantly impact the outcome of the next steps in the Consultative Selling Cycle

When trying to unravel needs, it must be done in a logical pattern that will bring the customer to a stage of realization that there is a problem or need.

So the art of uncovering needs requires the use of different types of questions. First let us have an understanding of the different types of questions that we could ask someone. Though there are several types of questions, for the purpose of this exercise let us look at just the 2 most important ones ie;

OPEN Questions

CLOSED Questions

Depending on what type of answer you want from the other person, either of these questions are used.

Eg; If I asked you: *Did you have your dinner'?*

Or *'Do you like this training session?'* or *'Are you going home this evening'?*

The only possible answer that you could give me would either be a *'yes'* or a *'no'*

That is why this type of Question is called a 'closed Question', because the only possible answer would be a one word- with either a *'yes'* or *'no'*

Closed questions usually begin with:

'Are you...'

'Will you...'

'Do you...'

'Would you...'

They are usually not very helpful in starting a conversation and extracting information. However, most sales people are more comfortable asking such questions, which we need to avoid at this stage.

The opposite of 'closed' is the obvious: 'open'.

Open questions allow the customer to open up or do the talking and are used to encourage a client to speak freely about a concern or expand on something already raised during the conversation

Always remember this: Open Questions generally begin with 5W's and 1 H ie;

Who?

What?

When?

Where?

Why?

How?

And they encourage the other person to open up and speak.

If we were to redo that example again using open questions, they would go something like this: *'What did you have for dinner?' 'How do you feel about this training?' 'What plans do you have for this evening'?*

These questions will certainly not fetch you a *'yes'* or *'no'* like how closed questions do. But they would allow the other person to open up with information which is what you as a sales person require.

Shooting out these questions without any logical order would also be inappropriate, as it could be unprofessional, could be irritating at times and most of all cause confusion in the mind of the customer. But if the customer was taken through a logical pattern, it could help lead him or open up to an understanding of his own situation, problem or need- that many times he may not be aware of.

There are two methodologies that could be used. Either of them is fine and would depend on which one you get more comfortable with. We recommend though, that the first method be used for simple, non complicated accounts, whilst the second method be used for complicated or major accounts.

The logical pattern for the first method mentioned usually starts with his '**Current Situation**' ...Questions like *'Where is the client now, Who is he dealing with, for how long and how satisfied is he'*?

This is where they are '**now**'. These questions are at most times factual and most times available either on their websites or from others around but are used to help start the conversation and build rapport. So we usually recommend that we do not ask many of these.

We then gradually move to the '**Desired Situation**' of where does the customer want to be or should be, with Questions like *'What would they like the ideal service levels to be or What would they like to see or have from an ideal vendor'*. The answers to these questions will tell us the customer's future plans or where they should be or want to be.

The next set of questions, are pertaining to the '**Barriers**' that are in his way, that are preventing him from reaching the desired situation. This is the key that will enable him open his eyes. Sometimes, just one question here could open up opportunities. Barrier questions most times begin with: *'What is preventing you from... "What is stopping you from...What is coming in the way to..."*

Here are some examples of these 3 types of Questions:

Current:
What are your upcoming Projects?
What is the current status of the Project?
How long have you been dealing with this Service Provider?

Desired:

What are your Customer's expectations?
How happy are you with the Service of the existing provider and what would you like it to be?
What are your expectations in having these resolved?
How do you plan to address these issues?
What would you like to happen to ensure a smooth working?

Barriers:

What are the factors coming in the way of you creating/maintaining a good brand Image?
What are the factors stopping you from maintaining a problem free situation?
What are the parameters which are preventing you to achieve......?

<u>EXERCISE</u>

Now keeping your customer in mind, look at building at least 5 questions each for '**Current**' and '**Desired**' and maybe 3 for '**Barriers**

Current

1.

2.

3.

4.

5.

Desired

1.

2.

3.

4.

5.

Barriers

1.

2.

3.

The second method as mentioned earlier is the **C.O.R.K.** Model- **C.O.R.K.** standing for: **C**urrent Circumstances, **O**bstacles, **R**epercussions and **K**ey for Solution.

You could start with the Current situation on the circumstances or Factual Questions, to help you start building a rapport to move on. Caution again here is not to ask too many of these Questions, since these are factual and it may seem or give the impression that you have not done prior work...So limit it to a few just to help you get started.

The next set of questions are the ones that can help open up on the Obstacles or Problems your customer is currently facing. Most times the customer will not even realize that they are sitting on a problem! Sometimes for years they could be living with this pain or problem without realizing. This is the real pain that his company could be going through. So effective Questions here can help him open up on this pain.

The third set of Questions deal with the Repercussions that these pains or problems could have or cause or lead to if not handled on time or not handled now! This creates the urgency for a change now! This is the subtle fear part that will help the customer make a change or decide to listen further to you.

The fourth set of Questions- the 'Key for Solution' is the step of asking the customer of what they think a good solution might be, which helps in promoting a platform for your solution and gain commitment from them on the usefulness of this proposed solution from you.

These four questions could be around the following key areas depending on your products or services:

- The Contacts or Decision Makers or Purchasing Process
- Current Supplier/Pricing
- Needs (long term/volume)
- The Organization size
- Special Delivery Requirements
- The Decision Making process
- Problems with Current Supplier (the Pain!)
- Problems this causes with other departments
- Other Problems

By being thorough in the preparation of your questions , which is usually done in advance at your preparation stage, you can ensure that nothing is missed and you can move to the next stage of the sales process with all the information you need.

We just covered a little earlier about the C.O.R.K. Model of Questioning. But I'd like to spend some more time on the 3 most important parts of this model- the **Obstacles,** the **Repercussion,** and **Key for Solution** set of Questions

Obstacle Questions are all about unraveling or probing about concerns, problems, pains, dissatisfactions or difficulties that the buyer is experiencing with the existing situation

Examples of this type of Question would be:

'What makes this operation difficult'?
'In what areas are you experiencing most difficulties'?
'What are some of the challenges you are experiencing with your existing supplier'?

Repercussion Questions are about the **consequences or effects** of a buyer's problems, difficulties, or dissatisfactions.

Once you have an indication or picture of the type of problem the customer is going through, you would now need to build or draw the customers' attention to the Repercussion or Effect that this problem could have if not acted on time.

Examples of this type of Question would be:
'What effect does that problem have on output'?
'Could that lead to added costs'?
'What happens if you do not achieve that goal'?
'Which other departments are effected'? Or 'Who all are effected with this'?

As you will see from the discussion that you have with the customer, several Implications can lead from one overriding problem or issue. Linking other possible problems or consequences to a given problem clearly increases its significance and urgency to the Buyer.

The 'Key for Solution' Questions will help you to get your customers to tell you the benefits that your solution can offer by asking them what they think a good solution might be, which can further help promote a platform for your solution and gain commitment from them on the usefulness of this proposed solution from you, when you move to the next step (Proving Value) of the Selling Cycle.

Examples of this type of Question would be:

'If you had to do ...., by how much would that save you'?'
'What would it mean to your customer service if you could have ....fitted or done'?
'What would it mean to your image and customer service if you could have......?

Here are some examples of the C.O.R.K. Model of Questions...focusing on the Current Circumstances, The Obstacles and the Repercussions. I hope that this will help give you a start in building your own list.

Circumstance Questions (Factual and most times can be used to build rapport-But don't waste time asking too many. These can usually be picked up from elsewhere prior to your meeting!)

- *What areas do you operate in?*
- *How many people work here?*
- *What is the ideal decision making process?*
- *What areas are you hoping to expand to?*

Obstacle Questions (Important!)

- *What criteria do your customers judge you on?*
- *What are the difficulties in working with....?*
- *Have you ever had a situation where you......*
- *What were some of the issues you've had to face in the past?*
- *What are issues you are facing in catering to your customer's expectations?*
- *How is your current service provider handling your...?*
- *What is your customer's feedback on the last project?*
- *What are the improvements you expect with the service that is currently offered?*
- *While looking for a new vendor what areas are given more priority?*
- *What areas you feel you are paying excess to your current service provider?*

Repercussion/ Impact Questions (Very Important!)

- *What happens when....?*
- *How much will that cost your organization?*
- *How big a problem will that be?*

- *Tell me......*
- *Explain.......*
- *Describe.....*
- *What effect does that issue have on your xxxx dept?*
- *How much will that cost you?*
- *How big a problem will that be?*
- *If this issue continues, what effects will that have on your......?*

Key for Solution Questions (Very important and leads you smoothly to the next step of the Sale ie; Proving Value)

- *What would it mean competitively, if you could just change or have......?*
- *How much better would the company image and your customer service be, if you could have...?*
- *By how much more would you be ahead of the competition if you had to....?*
- *If you had to do ...., by how much would that save you?*

Remember: As a Sales Professional, there are 5 important **P's** in Selling. Your job is to first of all uncover the **Problems, Pains** and **Predicaments**, and only after which these could give rise to the **Possibilities** for you to **Prescribe!**...Till then, you as the salesperson have no right to do so, and even if you do, this can drastically effect your credibility and future relationship. It is like a doctor trying to prescribe without diagnosing the case!

<u>EXERCISE</u>

Now keeping your customer in mind, look at building at least 5 questions each for '**Current Circumstances**', '**Obstacles**', '**Repercussions**' and '**Key for Solution**'

Current Circumstances

1.

2.

3.

4.

5.

Obstacles

1.

2.

3.

4.

5.

Repercussions

1.

2.

3.

4.

5.

Key for Solution

1.

2.

3.

4.

5.

What should the Sequential Pattern be in this stage?

1. A good way to begin is always start with Open Questions (Using either of the Questioning patterns mentioned above ie; Current, Desired, Barriers or Current Circumstances, Obstacles, Repercussions and Key for Solution)

2. Listen attentively

3. Take Notes

4. Clarify/ Reconfirm with Closed Questions

A Professional Salesperson ideally follows a sequential pattern at this stage, starting with Open Questions to uncover the Pain, Problems and their Repercussions and further follows it with Questions on the Key for Solutions.

While the customer talks, you as a Sales person would need to listen attentively.

'People were designed with two ears and one mouth, and that is the ratio in which to use them'!

How to be a good listener?

One of the greatest skills that you as a Sales Person can develop is the skill of listening. The best salespeople are the ones that do less talking and more of listening and that is why I believe God gave us two ears and one mouth- so we would do more listening than talking!

Here are some keys to be an "active" listener:

- Suspend judgment, initially- Keep an open mind
- Focus on the speaker and what he is saying including his body language
- Never interrupt while the customer speaks
- Tolerate silence. Silence can initially be uneasy, but if you practice tolerating it, you will find it very beneficial especially when negotiating.
- Listen for facts and key words
- Avoid distractions; when on the telephone don't carry on side conversations; when face-to-face make eye contact
- Assess what you've heard
- Take notes of key points
- Clarify and reconfirm what the customer has told you- never assume!
- Never use your phone in the customers' premises! It's a big disturbance and bad manners

Before you respond, assess the information you heard by asking yourself four questions in your mind:

- *What has the customer told me?*
- *What can I do with this information?*
- *What else do I need to know?*
- *What questions do I still need to ask?*

To show you're listening actively:

- Respond by using terms like, *'Go on', Uh huh'* and *'mmm'*
- Stay tuned in; Watch for non-verbal cues

To show that you have, understood:

- Use, phrases like *"I see,"* *"I understand"*
- Paraphrase, *"So you want me to ..."*

<u>EXERCISE</u>

What are areas that you would need to work on to improve your listening skills beginning from your very next call?

1.

2.

3.

4.

5.

6.

7.

8.

9.

10.

Taking Notes

A professional sales person will always takes notes of key points and never depend on memory.

By taking notes you are subtly telling the customer:

-I care about your business
-I do not want to miss anything
-The competition came by, but was more interested in the order- I am here to help!
-I am a professional

Clarifying and Reconfirming with Closed Questions

This is the time when closed questions are very useful. To clarify and reconfirm, restate in your own words what the client has said and ask him to verify your understanding. An example would be: *'Mr Customer, Let me just take a minute to summarize, just to ensure that I've got the right information…You were mentioning that you were having a problem with….Am I right Mr. So & So?"*

After the other person has confirmed your understanding, you have earned the right to proceed with additional questions to gain more information about the situation.

Why summarize regularly?

- *It keeps complexities under control*
- *It tests progress*
- *It lets you restate what the other party has said*
- *It can help gain the initiative*
- *It can keep the discussion on track*
- *It can prevent misinterpretation, misunderstanding and subsequent bitterness*
- *In other words, summarizing helps you stay on top (but you take the point).*

By summarizing, you are making sure you have the right information and that you haven't left out anything.

PROVING VALUE OF YOUR PRODUCTS/ SERVICES

The Fourth Step in the Consultative Selling Process and another very important step is Proving the Value of your Product or Service in the mind of the customer.

Usually the temptation for a Sales Person at this stage, once he's identified the need is to immediately jump into recommending the solution- This can backfire with a number of objections, as the customer is yet not convinced on the value of your proposition. Therefore, there is one more step, before we actually get to recommend your solution; to build in the mind of the customer the value that your company and the product or service that matches the relevant need identified brings to them.

It is similar to what a good waiter would do in a restaurant. Before he takes your order he would literally make your mouth water by talking about the taste of the dishes by building up that appetite in you. So now when he does bring the dish to the table, you are ready to relish it!

Proving value is the process of showing your client how specific features of your product or service can offer benefits that will help your customer meet a business need, solve a problem or realize an opportunity that you had identified in the earlier step.

The purpose of Proving value is to demonstrate to the client the value of your product or service.

Not all clients will be sure of the value; particularly new customers.

Proving value allows you to show the client why your product or service is an effective one and the value it brings to them, before you show the client how you can help them solve a problem/need or realize an opportunity with your recommendation.

Whenever people buy anything, there are two aspects that they are concerned about:

1. *What will the relevant product or service do for my company- how will it help me? What value will we get from this?*
2. *Who or Which is the company behind this? Their standing? Will they support me when I need them? The Reliability factor!*

Let us look at the Product or Service first:

There are 3 aspects to your products or services. The **Features, Advantages** and **Benefits**

A Feature describes some *'characteristics'* of a product or service. Features are relatively neutral, both in their content and in their effect on the buyer. Features are those aspects of a product, or service that we can see, or describe. It is usually what the manufacturer or producer *'has put into'* the product.

Example:
- *This mobile phone has a 'hands-free' facility*

When presenting features it is important to emphasize only those features that the customer said were most important to the customer during the probing phase of the sales process. These relate to the customers' buying criteria.

Now a number of Sales people lose out big time because they rattle 'only' the features of the product or service they are representing. And because of this the customer does not see the perceived value, because sometimes this could just sound technical and go over his head!

We need to translate the relevant feature into an ultimate Benefit. In other words *'what will it do'* for the customer!

Again, some sales people make the mistake of mentioning all of the features of the product or service that they could think of during their presentation.

This is not helpful at all, but on the contrary confusing and can actually deter the customer from making a positive buying decision. It can seem that the sales person wasn't listening effectively during the questioning phase of the sales process.

So as a Sales person, it is for you now to translate this relevant Feature or Features that you just spoke of into an Advantage

An Advantage describes how a product, or a product feature, can be used or can help the buyer during the buying process.

Advantages, as you will see are more persuasive than features. *Salespeople who talk about advantages sell more than salespeople who feature dump.*

Building on the same example:
- *Because this mobile has a hand-free facility, you can use it safely to answer calls, while driving when the car is in motion*

At this stage, we need to remind ourselves that people buy because they have needs.

If you as the seller can relate the product or service specifically to those needs identified in the earlier step, then there is a high probability of making a sale.

Benefits describe how the features and advantages will affect the buyer individually. They relate to the emotional buying behavior. In other words, the key is: ***what will the product or service do*** for them!

The key benefit words and statements are reassurance, confidence and peace of mind.

Asking questions in the earlier stage was to identify needs. Once we have identified the buyers' main buying criteria we can link the appropriate Features to the relevant Advantages and Benefits.

- Think **FAB!**

Going back now to our earlier example of the mobile phone...

- *Because our mobile has a hand-free facility you can be confident that if a customer calls you in the car, you can respond to the call quickly and safely and not miss out on vital enquiries or business opportunities.*

Every business has 5 main needs and your Benefit must address <u>one</u> or <u>more</u> of these ...

they are the **5** P's...

Profit- to make more money, that's why they are in business- savings, cost reductions etc

Protection- to ensure the security and safety of their business/ lives/ property etc,

Peace-A good night's sleep with no botheration or worry
Prestige-Wanting to stand out-Image! (for some!)
Performance- Improved productivity, more efficiency etc
In the example that we just covered, you will notice that the customer benefits by:
1. Business calls that could come in while he is driving: more revenue!
2. Safety while driving
3. To some- even prestigious using a 'hands-free' and driving

What is one phone call worth to him? If on an average he gets 10 business calls when driving, that could be the amount of business potential he could be missing out if not attended to. So now the customer begins to see value in this feature of the product.

It is like an 'FM Radio Frequency' existing between the Buyer and Seller!

'WII-FM'

It is like the customer always sending out signals of... **What Is In It For Me?**

And until this Question is answered by the sales person, the Customer will never proceed!

What to keep in Mind when working on Solutions...
The customer's vision-short term/ long term
The customer's key Challenges/ Pains and Requirements

Some examples might include:
Cost reduction;
Improvement in quality;
Improvement in end – user satisfaction;
Regulatory or legislation changes;
Capacity increase;
Innovation;
Reduction of customer's 'churn' (customers' moving away);
Increase in diversity of offering (adding new products or services);
Replacement of previous or incumbent supplier

<u>EXERCISE</u>

List all the relevant features of your product / service. Then translate each of the respective features into an Advantage and a Benefit.

REMEMBER: The relevant benefit must address the Question: *"What's in it for the Customer?"* And must address 1 or more of the 5 P's seen above.

<u>Features</u>	<u>Advantages</u>	<u>Benefits</u>
1.		
2.		
3.		
4.		
5.		

As mentioned, the other aspect of Proving Value has to do with the company that is backing the relevant product or service.

When Proving Value of your Company, it is important to keep in mind the USP's of your company– or 'Unique Selling Propositions'...*What is it that makes your company stand out from the others. What is so special about your company? Why should the customer move from his current vendor to deal with your company?*

Your USP's have to be strong enough for it to draw the customer to you!

Few pointers are suggested below that can help you think further:
-Stability of Company/ Expertise
-Years of Standing
-Special Service Features/ Capabilities
-Terms and Conditions
-Creativity
-Alliances and Partnerships
-Leveraging outside resources and partners network to service our clients
-Awards/ Recognitions

EXERCISE

Try listing as many USP's that you can think of that differentiates your company from the competition

1.

2.

3.

4.

5.

6.

7.

8.

9.

10.

STANDING OUT AND DIFFERENTIATING FROM THE COMPETITION!

This is an interesting Exercise you could undertake every time you are making a proposal to a customer.

As we have seen above, people make decisions based on what the product or service will do for them, along with the company backing this.

Keeping the Product/ Service and the company backing it, we can now say that customers would be ideally seeking **Value** on one hand and **Uniqueness** on the other.

So list all features of your offering that you think makes you **Unique** (from the customers' angle or perception) and the perceived **Value** to the Customer (ideally about 10 to 15)

S. No.	Feature	Uniqueness	Value
1.	Example 1	8	9
2.			
3.			
4.			
5.			
6.			
7.			
8.			
9.			
10			

Rate **Uniqueness** and **Value** respectively (on a 0 to 10 scale based on how you feel the customer perceives it)

Remember: What can be relevant for one client can be irrelevant for other clients!

Now plot them on a Quadrant with **Value** on **x axis** and **Uniqueness** on the other **y axis**

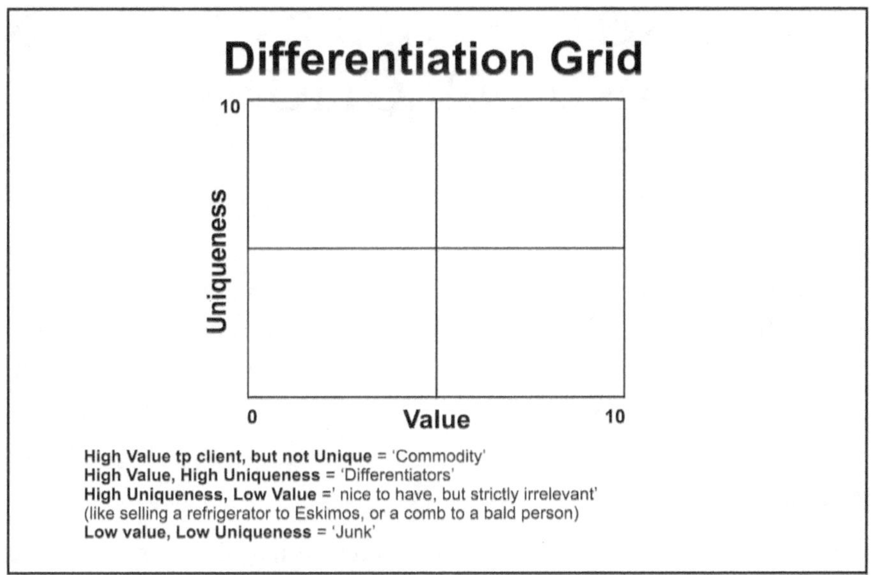

Illustration: How to differentiate your company from your competition

Once you've plotted these features on to the 4 quadrants, we now need to see what is of relevance, so we could use only those features that matter to the client, based on the need identified...

When its **High on Value** and **High on Uniqueness**- then these are your **key 'Differentiators'** (The ones appearing in the top right hand corner quadrant)

The features that are in this quadrant are the ones that <u>only you</u> are offering. These are your differentiators. If done really well, then this could indicate that this is what makes you stand out!

High on Value to the client, but **not Unique**, is a **'Commodity'** (the bottom right quadrant)

Any feature appearing in this quadrant is what your competition is also offering- just like you! Nothing great! When you start talking these features, you are on the same battle ground as your competition. The customer now compares you with others.

High Uniqueness and **Low in Value** could be 'nice to have, but strictly irrelevant' to the customer (Top left hand corner) – It does not make sense at all to the customer. The need and the relevant features are a mismatch (like trying to sell a fridge to Eskimos or a comb to a bald person!)

When it is **Low in Value** and **Low in Uniqueness**, just discard these as 'Junk'(Bottom left quadrant)-Don't even look at them or talk of them!

HANDLING CUSTOMER CONCERNS AND OBJECTIONS

An important component at this stage (or can happen earlier too) is: The Handling of Objections.

During the Sales Process, even the best salespeople can encounter objections that are difficult to handle. An objection is a concern or question raised by the client that delays or prevents you from proceeding to the next step in the Consultative Selling Cycle.

By using the right techniques, however, you can handle these objections without losing your focus.

Whenever I come to this part I am always reminded of why farmers place a 'scare- crow' in the middle of a paddy or rice field. The answer is obvious- to scare away the birds. But a clever bird knows that behind this so called 'scare-crow' are juicy grains- or his food!

So also, I believe, that a smart sales person knows that behind every objection there is a genuine need to buy! The objection in question must however be handled or cleared before progress is made.

Why do you think Customers raise objections?

During the sales process customers will raise objections for many reasons. At some stage, customers could:

- *Misunderstand something you have said.*
- *Feel pressurized.*
- *Are not convinced about your claims.*
- *Haven't yet made up their mind.*
- *Have to go back and justify their buying decision to others.*

One of the most common times objections are raised is just <u>before</u> the decision to purchase. In this case the customer is often looking for reassurance that the decision to buy is the right one.

We must understand however, that objections form a natural part of the buying process. Just before making a buying decision the buyer worries about making a mistake. And we all do this every day, even for the smallest purchase, so why get worked up when the customer does so?

So if an objection is raised at this stage, it means that the buyer has an unanswered question or concern that the salesperson has to deal with and it could most times be a positive rather than a negative situation when a customer raises an objection

Mostly, there are **two types** of objections that you will encounter:
Doubt
Indifference
Doubt, sometimes is referred to as distrust, and is expressed when the **client doesn't believe something you have said.**
Indifference on the other hand is expressed when **the client feels that what you have said is not important to him** – the client may simply feel that it is not appropriate to his situation.

Both type of objections occur for specific reasons. To overcome an objection, you need to recognize why it occurred and then deal with it, **immediately.**

Clarifying Objections

Clarify what the objection is (express empathy if appropriate)

Then respond accordingly:

- To remove doubt:

    a. Refer to a similar situation and/or

    b. Offer evidence or proof that what you have said is true

- To handle indifference:

    c. If based on a misunderstanding or lack of information, explain your point more thoroughly and or

    d. Outweigh the indifference with the benefits of your suggested approach

Now we need to deal with the objection: Once you fully understand the nature of the objection then it can be answered in different ways depending on whether it is

- ✓ a misunderstanding by the customer
- ✓ disbelief over claims you are making
- ✓ a product disadvantage.

You will now need to verify that the objection is removed or cleared from the mind of the customer and to ensure it does not come up later.

Your next step would be to Advance the sale.

The key to objection handling is to react less quickly when an objection is raised and find out more about the problem. Clarify exactly what the problem is then try to overcome the objection.

Finally, if you have dealt with the objection successfully and it is the right time, close the sale, or move on to the next stage of the sales process.

EXERCISE

Before we go any further, list down all the possible objections you have come across so far or you come across regularly (Whatever comes to your mind):

1.

2.

3.

4.

5.

6.

7.

8.

9.

10

Most objections or customer concerns can broadly be classified under **4 key heads,** as you will see in the illustration.

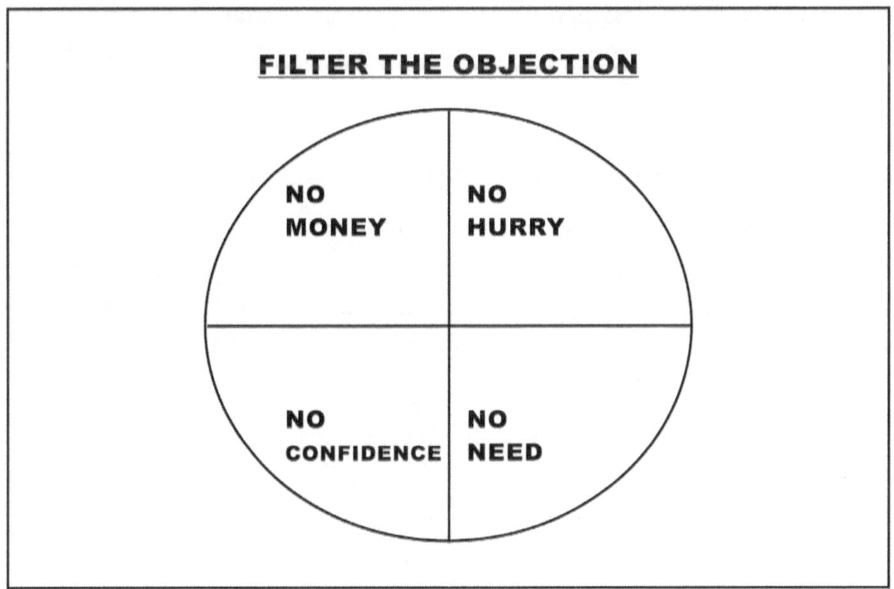

Illustration: Filtering your Objections

Now try to classify under which quadrant each of your objections (you listed above in the Exercise) fall in under:

For example; If a customer says: *'Your rates are too high'* or *'You guys are very costly'*

Obviously this would feature under the quadrant '**NO MONEY**'

Another example for 'NO MONEY': *'I need a discount!'*

'I don't want to deal with your company again. I had a bad experience last year'!

Or *'Never heard of your company...not too sure about them'!*

Examples like the two above will fall in under the '**NO CONFIDENCE**' Quadrant.

An example of what would come under the quadrant of '**NO HURRY**' would be something like this: *'I am fairly happy with what we have now. We could possibly look at this later only'*

Or *'I don't need any changes right now'* or *'We have enough of this for now'*

The last quadrant '**NO NEED**' is a little tricky and could be something like this: We are n*ot interested'* or *'Please don't see me again'* or *'I don't need you guys'*

Now once you have classified all your objections under the four respective quadrants, let us see what each means and how to go about handling them.

NO MONEY

Do you think the Customer really does not have that additional money?

What he is actually conveying to you by raising that concern that falls in this quadrant is that he does not really see value in your proposition. And most times it will be that the sales person has been rattling off features of his product or service, without really proving value of how the customer will benefit or what it would do for him.

TIP: Keep 'FAB' in mind. Prove value by translating the relevant features to benefits. What is in for the customer? What will it do for him- translate into tangible benefits that he can see, that far outweighs what he would be investing in.

NO CONFIDENCE

There could be 2 scenarios here:

1. A past customer who has had bad experience and now no more wants to deal with you
2. A new customer who has never heard of you and doubts your company's capability

If it is a past customer, how would we go about building his confidence again in your company and service?

TIP: Show them testimonials of satisfied customers in the same business as theirs, site visits to such customers, case stories of how you resolved similar cases and the outcome, have them connect on phone right away with customers who will talk well of you etc. You could also build on the USP's of your company, particularly relevant to his company and need

If it is a new customer, who has never heard of your company and doubts its capability, then how would we go about instilling and building his confidence in your company and service?

TIP: This is where the USP's prepared under the step Proving Value will help. You could highlight the USP's of your company particularly relevant to his company and need. Show them testimonials of satisfied customers in the same business as theirs, site visits to such customers etc. Particularly of interest would be your Credibility, Standing in the Market, your After-Sales-Support and Financial Status.

NO HURRY

How do we get the customer to take or commit on a decision now?
TIP: Look at what incentives you have now that the customer could benefit by.
What if your company does not have the required material when he requires?
With the costs of raw materials, labour etc going up, what is the guarantee that he would get your product/ services at this same rate?

NO NEED

Any objection falling in this quadrant is probably one of the most difficult. There are 2 possibilities:

1. There is genuinely no need- He may not be a likely customer
2. He has a need but has not disclosed

If it is the second scenario, then we will need to go back to step 3 of the Selling Skills plan which is Fact-finding or Probing to uncover further. If the customer is still unwilling to reveal, then in most times it could be something personal about you as an individual that he is put off with.

TIP: Allow a few days for him to cool down, and then have someone senior from your organization visit them to build up again

Handling the PRICE Objection

Price is probably one of the most common objections we hear in sales. Customers will say *'you are too expensive'*, but before we react, we need to think about what it might mean when they say so.

Sadly, most sales people respond immediately with a *'No Sir....'* rather than trying to understand what was in the customers mind when he said this!

You need to put yourself in the Clients Shoes!

Perceptions Differ! We need to specifically understand...
How short is short!
How firm is firm!
How slim is slim!

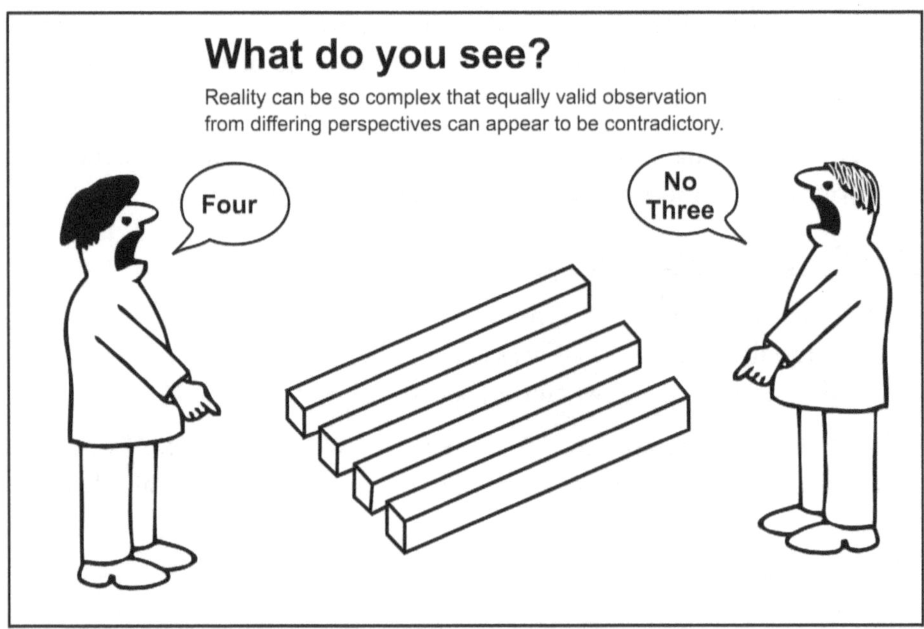

Illustration: Perceptions Differ!

As seen from the 2 illustrations on the previous page, perceptions of individuals differ. So all the more it makes sense to clarify the customers understanding of *'prices are high'* or *'too expensive'* before we hastily jump into handling the same

Too expensive could mean several of these and more:

- *I've had another quote*
- *I'm checking you out*
- *I'm negotiating with you*
- *I have to go back and convince others*
- *It's more than I expected*
- *It's more than I have in my budget*
- *I don't want to buy from you*

This is why it is so important to clarify this objection before we attempt to handle it. We need to find out the real reasons behind the objection. Often we react too quickly and give what we feel is the right answer, but in fact we could be totally wrong.

The customer may have had another quote and may have constituents to satisfy. They may be looking for help etc. Interrupting or not clarifying but giving an inappropriate answer will not help the customer achieve their buying objectives.

Steps to handling an Objection

One of the best ways to answer any sales objection is to:

1. Listen to the objection: Resist the temptation of interrupting the customer. You may have heard the objection a hundred times but not from this particular customer. It may also be that the customer has more than one objection, or that this particular objection is slightly different than the ones you usually hear.

2. Prevent further objections arising: Actually one great way to ensure that this objection never surfaces again or another one does not come up again after you've handled the first one is to ask a question that could go something like this: *'Mr Customer, before I go into answering this concern for you...let me clarify...Is this the only concern that is preventing you from moving forward?'*

    In most case the customer will say *'Oh, Yes'*. Now what you've actually done is to indirectly prevent him from coming up with any further excuses in the future!

3. Filter the Objection: See which of the 4 quadrants of NO MONEY, NO HURRY, NO CONFIDENCE, NO NEED (covered above) it falls into

4. If Price, clarify the objection: To clarify the objection you could say something like: *"When you say we are expensive, could you be a little more specific?"*

    Listen to what the customer says. He would then clarify why he feels you are expensive. Based on his answer you could take forward. If he is comparing you with the competition, then use your differentiation grid (covered earlier) to stand out.

In closing this chapter I'd like to use a quote that I stumbled upon the other day, that is called I believe "**The Common Law of Business Balance**" which is a meditation on price and is attributed to **John Ruskin** – a 19th century English poet, fervent art critic, and socialist.

> *'There is hardly anything in the world that some man cannot make a little worse and sell a little cheaper. People who consider price only are this man's lawful prey.*
> *It's unwise to pay too much, but it's unwise to pay too little.*
> *When you pay too much you lose a little money; that is all.*
> *When you pay too little, you sometimes lose everything, because the thing you bought was incapable of doing the thing you bought it to do.*
> *The common law of business balance prohibits paying a little and getting a lot.*
> *It can't be done.*
> *If you deal with the lowest bidder, it's well to add something for the risk you run.*
> *And if you do that, you will have enough to pay for something better.*

PROVIDING YOUR RECOMMENDATION/ SOLUTION

We are now at the Fifth Step of the Selling Process, which is the Recommendation Stage

Actually, if you have brought the customer right up to here, you will realize that this particular step is a mere formality of wrapping up the entire discussion.

Recommending may follow Proving Value with some customers (for example to new customers) or can happen immediately after Fact-Finding with other clients that have already dealt with your company (who are familiar with the features and benefits you have to offer)

The purpose of Recommending is to show the client the specific product features and benefits which will solve their needs / problems. It is the process of presenting your specific product or service solution to fulfill one or more needs identified during Fact Finding

Steps

- Summarize the client's needs(s)/problem(s)

- Recap the Value from your product/ service related to the need(s)/ problem(s)

- Recommend the appropriate Solution

CLOSING THE SALE

Closing is the **Sixth** and **Final Step** in the Consultative Selling Cycle.

It is the focal point of the cycle and it involves obtaining the client's commitment to take a suggested action.

The purpose of this step is to obtain the client's commitment to take the action that you have suggested or recommended.

In fact, if you've done till here, following all the steps outlined so far, you will invariably find the customer ready and already agreeing with you!

<u>So what then prevents Salesmen from Closing?</u>

- Many sales people are looking for 'closing techniques' that will make the decision making process easier and take away some of the pressure felt by both buyer and seller at that moment of truth, when a decision is about to be made.

- The problem is that at this point the salesperson is worried about getting rejected and how he will have to face his boss back in the office, whilst the buyer is worried about making a mistake. So it is all too easy for either, or both sides to delay the buying decision, rather than risking rejection, or taking the wrong decision

It is up to you as the sales person to have the confidence, at the right time, to ask for a commitment and risk rejection. That is your role and unfortunately, 7 times out of 10 salesmen fail to ask for some kind of commitment and this can make them lose the sale they have been working on so hard to achieve- by allowing the competition to come in at this stage. All their hard work is eaten up by the competition. .

Research has shown that 70% of sales contacts end up with the salesperson not asking for a commitment, or an order as the case maybe.

Fear of rejection takes over and we miss the opportunity to close. While many sales people see closing as being about techniques this is not actually the main issue.

Closing is about <u>**timing**</u> rather than **techniques**.

So what then is 'Closing'?

The sales process is about seeking out problems and trying to identify solutions. We cannot close the customer, or gain some sort of commitment from them until there is an identified need for our solution.

- It used to be said in the earlier days '**ABC of Selling**'- meaning to "**Always be closing**" but this approach does not fit in with relationship selling.
- The right time to close is when the customer is ready to buy.
- If the salesperson is always trying to close this will irritate most customers and they will probably reject the salesperson- this is also one of the reasons why this is the most hated profession as seen earlier.
- Closing is about timing, not technique. The best way to sell is to make it easy for the customer to buy.
- The close is important and we should have the confidence to ask for the order at the appropriate time. However, we must put the close into perspective and keep selling simple.

A few Important Points about Closing

Closing the sale is an integral part of the sales process:

Before a buyer will place an order with you, he or she will have to see a need for your product and be convinced that your particular product represents the best solution to the problem represented by that need.

No salesperson ever closed every sale:

Everyone who has ever sold professionally has had to get used to living with rejection. A good salesperson will always be rejected more times than he or she is successful. Every time you fail, you move closer to the time you will succeed.

Selling is a 'numbers game':

Given a 'basic' level of skill in sales techniques, the amount you sell is directly related to the number of calls you make. The more customers you see, the more business you will close.

Certain key ratios apply to your sales activity:

By measuring your sales performance over a period of time you will understand more fully the key ratios that apply to your business

The right time to close is when the customer is ready to buy:

This is so important. Closing tends to happen towards the end of the sales call but don't assume this will always be the case. If the customer wants to buy early into your sales presentation then you should get a commitment straight away.

Look for more than one opportunity to close the sale:

There will be several occasions during the sale when the customer is ready to buy. There will also be more than one opportunity for you to close the sale.

Buyer resistance is natural and should be expected:

Often when the buyer hesitates during the closing stages he or she is seeking reassurance from the salesperson in a consultative, non-threatening way, that the decision that is about to be made, is a good decision.

Buyers seldom ask you for the order:

Most buyers rely on the salesperson to make the buying process easy for them. However, they rarely ask for the order outright so the most effective and most obvious closing technique, having gone through the several stages of the call, is to ask the buyer if he or she wishes to place an order.

Some suggestions to help you Close

The easiest and most effective close is to:

Ask for the order It has been estimated that 7 out of every 10 sales contacts end without the salesperson asking for the order, or some form of commitment. This is due either to lack of confidence, or fear of rejection.

The Assumptive close uses a question that is phrased in a way that assumes the customer is going ahead with the sale. Eg: *When/Where will you want delivery?*

The Alternative close gives a choice between two positive alternatives. Closing on a small issue is about choosing a minor feature of your product or service and gaining agreement from the buyer on that feature. Eg: *Will you prefer us to start Tue or Wed?*

The Pressure close enables you to put pressure on the buyer in terms of special offers or inducements that are available or penalties for not placing the order. Eg: *This price is only available up to the end of this month.*

Converting on Objections: An objection can be a very strong buying signal. If the buyer raises an objection and it is the only objection that is preventing the order from being placed you can use this to gain commitment to buy.

Eg: *You have said Mr. Buyer that you are interested in our services, but the schedule that we are talking of is unacceptable to you. Is this the only concern you have? If we are able to work out a compromise would you be willing to place an order today?*

The Negotiated close: Standard negotiating techniques are very useful at the closing stages of the sales process.

Eg: If *I am able to reduce my price by 10% will you agree today?* (can be used for delivery also!)

The Trial or Test close is used during your presentation and gets feedback from the customer on what they have heard so far.

 Eg: Listen to what the buyer says, summarize what has been said and ask for the order/ close the sale

Do you have all the information on which to make a decision?

The Choice close: Gives two or more alternatives. Eg: *"May I send you an email of the order we have discussed or would you prefer to have me stop by tomorrow?"*

Finally, the **balance sheet method** is used where you are in direct competition with another company. List all the points in favor of your product and all the points against on sheet of paper.

This is repeated for the competitor product. If your product is the stronger of the alternatives available to the buyer this method can help the final decision be made in your favor.

After asking for the order, just **shut up!** (I have seen many sales personnel messing up at this stage by opening their mouths on something irrelevant and allowing the customer to go off on a tangent- thereby delaying or postponing and sometimes even losing the sale all together!)

Finally, the experience of bagging an order, whatever be the size usually gives every sales person a joyous feeling and the word **'SALE'** says it all:

S - Such

A - A

L - Lovely

E - Experience!

TIPS TO NEGOTIATE EFFECTIVELY

What is Negotiation?

The authors of '*Getting to Yes*' define negotiating as a *"back-and-forth communication designed to reach an agreement when you and the other side have some interests that are shared and others that are opposed."*

A lot of people hate negotiations, not realizing that we negotiate every day, on a regular basis. Most of us face different types of negotiations throughout our personal and professional lives...

During an average day, we may negotiate with:

- ✓ The boss, regarding an unexpected work assignment;
- ✓ Subordinates, regarding unexpected overtime;
- ✓ A supplier, about a problem with raw materials etc;
- ✓ A banker, over the terms of a business loan;
- ✓ A government official, regarding the compliance with environmental regulations;
- ✓ A real estate agent, over the lease on a new warehouse;
- ✓ Your spouse, over who will walk the dog;
- ✓ Your child, over who will walk the dog (still an issue after losing the previous negotiation!);

Our ability to negotiate has been embedded since we were born.

Remember, as a child when you wanted a particular toy and your mum or dad said '*No!*' What did you do next? You cried...you brought the roof down, till you got that toy!

So as we can see, negotiation is a common, everyday activity that most people use to influence others and to achieve personal objectives. In fact, negotiation is not only common, but also essential to living an effective and satisfying life. We all need things- resources, information, cooperation, and support from others. Others have those needs as well, sometimes compatible with ours, sometimes not.

Negotiation is therefore a process by which we attempt to influence others to help us achieve our needs while at the same time taking their needs into account.

People often think about negotiation as just a method of getting their way. But it's really all about relationships.

The need for negotiation comes about because of a conflict of interests. What you want isn't what I want. But because we need to maintain a relationship, we decide to talk about our differences instead of walking away or beating each other up.

We search for a solution to our conflict of interests. We negotiate. And in the end, if the negotiation is successful, we get a solution we can both live with.

It may not be perfect. You may not get all you want, and neither may I. But it's better than what we would have had if we hadn't negotiated and continued in conflict.

<u>**Exercise:**</u>

Here is a small challenge that I would like to start off with, to help you understand this subject more:

A father left 17 Camels as an Asset for his Three Sons. When the Father passed away, his sons opened up the will. The Will of the Father stated that:

-The Eldest son should get Half of 17 Camels (1/2),
-The Middle Son should be given 1/3rd of 17 Camels,
-The Youngest Son should be given 1/9th of the 17Camels

As it is not possible to divide 17 into half or 17 by 3 or 17 by 9, the sons started to fight with each other

Can you help them solve this!

(Go ahead...have a try before you see the solution below)

Solution:

They decided to go to a wise man. The wise man listened patiently about the Will. The wise man, after giving this thought, brought one camel of his own and added the same to 17. That increased the total to 18 camels.

Now, he started reading the deceased father's will.
- ✓ Half of 18   = 9. *So he gave 9 camels to the eldest son*
- ✓ 1/3rd of 18 = 6. *So he gave 6 camels to the middle son*
- ✓ 1/9th of 18 = 2. *So he gave 2 camels to the youngest son*

Now add this up: 9 + 6 + 2 = 17
- ✓ So this leaves 1 camel-which the wise man took back.

Here's the Lesson for you as a Negotiator!
The attitude of negotiation and problem solving is to **find the 18th camel- ie; <u>the common ground.</u>**
Once a person is able to find <u>**the common ground**</u>, the issue is resolved. It is difficult at times. However, to reach a solution, the first step is to believe that **<u>there is a solution.</u>**

If we think that there is no solution, we won't be able to reach any!

<u>**Exercise:**</u>

1. Look at 2 Examples: One Personal and another Official

2. Reflect on what was the MOST Challenging Experience you had in negotiating something?

(How did you come about? What made it successful? What do you think you needed if not successful?)

Exercise:
Think of a Great Negotiator!
What Skills or Attributes does he/ she possess?
1.
2.
3.
4.
5.
6.
7.
8.
9.
10.

Some of the Skills and Attitudes observed in TOP Negotiators are:

Attitude	Skills
Commitment	Time management
Customer	Commercial awareness
Passion of energy	Team working
Determination	Ability to present ideas in writing
Self Motivation	Innovation- creative & flexible
Patience	Strategist- Prepares & Plans
Empathy	Effective Communicator
Resilience	
Belief/ Confidence	

Exercise:
List some of the Key **Attitudes**, **Skills** and **Habits** that you possess for a Negotiator?
1.
2.
3.

4.

5.

6.

7.

8.

List some of the **Attitudes, Skills** and **Habits** that you lack or are weak in and need to work on?

1.

2.

3.

4.

5.

What will you do to improve? By when?
Action Plan

————————————————————————————————

————————————————————————————————

————————————————————————————————

————————————————————————————————

NEGOTIATION QUESTIONS TO ASK YOURSELF- PREPARATION CHECKLIST

1. What do I want from this negotiation? What are my Objectives: Outcome?
    Must Achieve
    Intend to
    Like to
2. What options or alternatives would be acceptable to me? What are the other sides' objectives?
3. How does the other side see the negotiation?
4. What are my strengths—values, skills, and assets—in this negotiation?
5. What are my weaknesses and vulnerabilities in this negotiation?
6. Why is the other party negotiating with me?
    What is it that I have & they have?
    What is it that I have & they do not?
    What is it that I need more?
    What is it that the other side needs more?
7. What are the lists of Variables/ Concessions from your side?
8. What are the lists of Variables/ Concessions from the Customers' side?
9. How am I going to achieve my objectives in this negotiation?
10. What is the strategy of the other side likely to be?
11. What tactics should I use within the negotiation?
12. What tactics is the other side likely to use?
13. What lessons can I apply from past negotiations to improve my performance?
14. Where and when should the negotiation take place?
15. How long should talks last? What deadlines are we facing?
16. What are my interests in the upcoming negotiation? How do they rank in importance?

17. What is my *best alternative to a negotiated agreement*, or BATNA? That is, what option would I turn to if I'm not satisfied with the deal we negotiate or if we reach an impasse? How can I strengthen my BATNA?

18. What is my *reservation point*—my indifference point between a deal and no deal?

19. What is my *aspiration point* in the negotiation—the ambitious, but not outrageous, goal that I'd like to reach?

20. What are the other side's interests? How important might each issue be to them?

21. What do I think their reservation point and BATNA may be? How can I find out more? Who can help?

22. Who has more power to walk away?

23. Is there a *zone of possible agreement* (ZOPA) between my reservation point and the other side's? If there clearly is no room for bargaining, then there's no reason to negotiate—but don't give up until you're sure. You may be able to add more issues to the discussion.

24. What is my relationship history with the other party? How might our past relationship affect current talks?

25. Are there other differences that we should prepare for?

26. In what order should I approach various parties on the other side?

27. What is the hierarchy within the other side's team? What are the patterns of influence and potential tensions? How might these internal dynamics affect talks?

28. What potential ethical pitfalls should we keep in mind during the negotiation?

29. Who are my competitors for this deal? How do our relative advantages and disadvantages compare?

30. What objective benchmarks, criteria, and precedents will support my preferred position?

31. Who should be on my negotiating team? Who should be our spokesperson? What specific responsibilities should each team member have?

32. Do we need to involve any third parties (agents, lawyers, mediators, influencers, interpreters)?

33. What authority do I have (or does our team have) to make firm commitments?

34. Have I practiced/ role-played communicating my message to the other side? How are they likely to respond?

35. Does the agenda make room for simultaneous discussion of multiple issues?

What other questions would you add to this negotiation preparation checklist?

<u>Negotiation Checklist:</u>

Here's a systematic way to ensure you are well-prepared before your next negotiation

❑ ✓ Item accomplished

A. About You

❑ 1. What is your overall goal?

❑ 2. What are the issues?

❑ 3. How important is each issue to you?

Develop a scoring system for evaluating offers:

❑ (a) List all of the issues of importance from step 2.

❑ (b) Rank-order all of the issues.

❑ (c) Assign points to all the issues (assign weighted values based on a total of 100 points).

❑ (d) List the range of possible settlements for each issue. Your assessments of realistic, low, and high expectations should be grounded in industry norms and your best-case expectation.

❑ (e) Assign points to the possible outcomes that you identified for each issue.

❑ (f) Double-check the accuracy of your scoring system.

❑ (g) Use the scoring system to evaluate any offer that is on the table.

❑ 4. What is your "best alternative to a negotiated agreement" (BATNA)?

❑ 5. What is your resistance point (i.e., the worst agreement you are willing to accept before ending negotiations)? If your BATNA is vague, consider identifying the minimum terms you can possibly accept and beyond which you must recess to gather more information.

B. About the Other Side

❑ 1. How important is each issue to them (plus any new issues they have added)?

❑ 2. What is their best alternative to negotiated agreement (BATNA)?

❑ 3. What is their resistance point?

❑ 4. Based on questions B.1, B.2, and B.3, what is your target/ goal?

C. The Situation

❑ 1. What deadlines exist? Who is more impatient?

❑ 2. What fairness norms or reference points apply?

❑ 3. What topics or questions do you want to avoid? How will you respond if they are asked anyway?

D. The Relationship between the Parties

❑ 1. Will negotiations be repetitive? If so, what are the future consequences of each strategy, tactic, or action you are considering?

❑ 2. Can you trust the other party? What do you know about them?

❑ 4. Does the other party trust you?

❑ 3. What do you know of the other party's styles and tactics?

❑ 4. What are the limits to the other party's authority?

❑ 5. Check in advance with the other party about the agenda.

A Quick Glance at Negotiation

Set Objectives: Outcome

Must Achieve

Intend to

Like to

Options/ Alternatives acceptable
Other sides Objectives

Information

What is it that I have & they have
What is it that I have & they do not
What is it that I need more
What is it that the other side needs more

Concessions/ Variables- Cost/ Value

Price

Delivery

Schedule

Place

Training

Payment

Add-ons etc

Trade concessions reluctantly

Optimize yours
Minimize theirs

Strategy

What is your Strategy? Have you role-played?

Tasks

If as a team, who will do what? When? At what stage?

Aim High

Keep whole package in mind

Silence! Sometimes it is best to **SHUT!**

During the closing stages you may need to find a negotiated solution that satisfies both parties.

As seen, Negotiating is not just about giving things away. It is about trading concessions to reach agreement. Most times a sales person will find that negotiating involves price issues.

The customer uses the price objection to gain a price reduction. If you have to give a reduction in price, always try to make it sound difficult and get something back in return

For Example: The customer says: "*Give me 10% discount and we have a deal*"

- The temptation, as a salesperson is to agree and secure the sale. A good negotiator would react differently and try to win a concession.

- "*This is extremely difficult, but if I am able to look at our discount structure, and if we were to go down that route I would then need a 2 year contract. Would that be possible?*"

- If the customer agrees two year contract is possible, then we can offer 10%, or perhaps less

AT-A-GLANCE-SUMMARY OF THE 6 STEP SELLING PLAN

- **Preparation**

Self- Mental/ Physical

Client Info (including Creditworthiness)

Market/ Industry/ Competition

Sales Tools

Your Strategy

- **Approach**

Salutation

Self

Company/Product

Convenient time

Purpose of call

Qualify for Authority: (Use: WANTS, FAINT or BANT)

Interest Creating Remark

Permission to move to next step

- **Fact-Finding (Uncovering Needs)**

(Use General Questions / Specific Questions/ Get customers' participation)

The step should identify the customer's

- Current Situation
- Desired Situation
- Existing Barriers

Questions to unravel: Pain, Problems & Predicaments.

Use the C.O.R.K. Model

Questions on:

- Market
- Competition(current supplier/rates)
- His future /long term plans

Listen and Take Notes

Paraphrase with Closed Questions

- **Proving Value**

Talk of your service

Link the features to the benefit and what's in it for them (sell Benefits!)

Relate Benefits to needs identified through Fact finding

Use visuals/ Create a movie in customers mind

Create desire

- **Recommendation**

Provide the product as a solution to the need that has been identified.

Answer customer concerns/ Handle Objections

Clear all doubts

- **Close-by asking for the order or obtaining a commitment!**

POST- MORTEM OF YOUR CALL

Evaluating your own Call

As a Professional it is of key importance that you build a system of Self-Coaching, to help you keep constantly working on your Competencies and Performance. It is based on the principle of: *'What I say to myself, is more important than what others say to me'*

You could, after every major call use the format shown below to evaluate the steps of your sales call. Keep doing this on a regular basis to ensure the bar moves from left to right for each specific step or area of your call

<u>Role Play- Observation Sheet</u>:   Name:...

FACTS COMMENTS Steps	Good	Average	Poor	EVALUATION on STANDARDS Specially what I did/saw/heard

<u>Preparation</u>
      -Mental/Self Image
-Account:
      -Client (including Credit)
      -Market/Industry/ Competition
      -Sales Tools
      -Strategy (Questions/Concerns)
    <u>Approach</u>
-Introduction-Salutation
      -Self/Co (H. Shake/ B. Card)
      -Convenient Time
      -ICR
      -Permission to move
 <u>Fact Finding</u>
-Builds Rapport
-Checks Decision Maker
-Questions
 Current/Desired/ Barriers
(…to uncover Pain Areas/ Problems)
      -Circumstances/ Current
      -Obstacles/ Pain
      -Repercussions/ Impact
      -Key for Solutions
-Listening Skills
-Note Taking
-Summarizes with Closed Questions
    <u>Proving Value</u>
-USP of Company
-FAB of Product
-Uses Differentiation Grid
-Handles Objections/Concerns
-Recognizes client agreement
    <u>Recommends & Closes</u>
-Summarizes Need/ Problem identified
-Recommends Appropriate Solution
-Shows how business needs will be met
-Negotiates Effectively
-Thanks Customer
    <u>Professional Demeanor</u>
Attitude
Assertive/ Confidence
Tone of voice
Use of language
Personal Grooming
    <u>Other Comments</u>

POST CALL-WIN OR LOSE, STAY PROFESSIONAL!

"And the Winner is..." Whether you win or lose- What next?

After Your Business Proposal Presentations-Follow Up!
On return, write a letter to all of the attendees:

- *Thank them*
- *Summarize the main points raised, and important conclusions.*
- *Clarify any points which the presentation revealed your client might find unclear*
- *Summarize the "next steps or course of action" you agreed, noting any time-scales decided upon.*
- *Outline as many reasons as you possibly can for maintaining ongoing contact with anyone involved in the assessment cycle.*
- *Put yourself "at their disposal" for any problems they have with, or questions they have.*

Some basic questions you could ask!

General
Who won?
How many bids or vendor presentations were received?
What was your overall score?
Was your score closer to the top or close to the bottom?
What was the winner's score?
Did the winner have the lowest price?
Did the winner have a higher score on the technical evaluation factors?

Price
If price was a major factor and you lost- Why and how?

Technical Reasons
If you scored higher on technical factors but lost- Reason?
If you scored lower on technical factors- How did your other factors score?
How did the Competition score? What did they have extra or do extra?

Competition

If the other party won- on what basis did they do so? Where did they score more?

Further Questions to ask the customer that can help in future

-Can you detail the particular factors that prompted you to select the successful bidder?

If these factors had been present in our proposal, would you have been prepared to do business with us? If not, why?

-How else would you suggest that we might have improved our chances of coming out of the proposal evaluation better and winning your business?

-What areas would you like to see changed in our organization that can be helpful to both our organizations?

-Would you be prepared to give us copies of non-proprietary parts of the successful vendor's proposal to allow us to more closely analyze why their bid was more successful, helping us to address any shortcomings in our approach to winning future business with your organization? (Don't be shy of asking for this sort of material – many clients will provide this valuable input to your competitive analysis).

-Are you prepared to consider us for any future business that might arise? (And if not, why not?)

-Are there any other current requirements that we might be able to help you with?

-Can we stay in touch with you to keep you informed of developments with our company and offerings?

Whatever you do...Do have a Professional Approach and
Attitude-at all times!
IT PAYS!

RETAINING YOUR CUSTOMERS FOR LIFE
IMPORTANCE OF GREAT CUSTOMER SERVICE!

This book on Professional Selling Skills will not be complete without the topic of Customer Service. Many Sales People today think that Customer Service is different from Sales. While this may be so, we must remind ourselves that every single person in the organization from the topmost person right to the lowest in rank can effect or have an impact on customers, by the way they treat them and therefore must have the *'hat'* of a Customer Service Professional too.

No business today can afford to ignore two very important people- **2C's** -**Your Customer** and **Your Competitor!** The person in front of you is your Customer, and if this person is not treated well, then the person behind you (Your Competitor!) is just waiting to grab him as he drops from your list!

So what then is this **Customer Service or Experience?**

Customer Service or their Experience is the customers' perception of how your company treats them. These perceptions affect their behaviors and build memories and feelings that will drive their loyalty. In other words: if they like you and continue to like you, they are going to do business with you and recommend you to others.

And for your customers to like you, you should know them very well to create and deliver personalized experiences that will entice their loyalty. But gaining this in-depth knowledge about customers isn't something that just happens. You as the Sales Person will need to work on this with your Customer. No doubt, this is well worth the effort.

And it doesn't matter what kind of business you are in – improving the experience for your customers is the key to increasing retention, satisfaction and sales.

Here are some vital data that can help you look at this area of your job on priority

1. *For consumers, customer experience will become more important than price and product by 2020.*
2. *89% of businesses compete through the level of customer experience they're able to deliver.* -Gartner

3. *70% of the customer's journey is dictated by how the customer feels they are being treated. -*McKinsey

4. *Businesses that deliver better customer experiences obtain revenues between 4% and 8% above their market. -*Bain & Company

5. *55% of customers are willing to spend more money with a company that guarantees them a satisfying experience. –*Think Jar

6. *70% of unhappy customers whose problems are resolved are willing to shop with a business again. -*Glance

7. *Customer service stats show that new customers cost anywhere between 5 and 25 times more than retaining existing customers. -*Harvard Business Review

8. *44% of consumers take their business elsewhere due to a poor experience. –*NewVoiceMedia

9. *50% of customers switch brands when their needs are not met.*

10. *13% of customers tell 15 people or more if they have a negative experience.* - Esteban Kolsky

11. *After one negative experience, 51% of customers will never do business with that company again.* - NewVoiceMedia

12. *72% of customers will tell 6 people or more if they have a satisfying experience.* - Esteban Kolsky

13. *67% of customers report a bad customer experience as the reason for switching businesses. -*Esteban Kolsky

14. *Only 1 in 26 customers will tell a business about their negative experience; the rest simply leave according to customer service facts. -*Esteban Kolsky

15. *79% of customers who share their complaints online see their complaints ignored. -*RightNow

As a Sales Professional, think of all the benefits to YOU and YOUR Organization by providing great Customer Service?

1.
2.
3.
4.
5.
6.

7.

8.

9.

10.

Customers usually don't care about what good you do! On an average when a customer is happy with a product or service, they would generally tell around 7 people, but if the service was bad or if they were disappointed with it, guess how many they would tell on an average?

Without considering the internet, the answer is 38 (just lip service)! But today, with almost everyone in possession of a mobile phone having an internet connection, you do not have to guess the figure!!!

Bad News certainly travels faster than Good News! You don't have to look far...See today's newspaper headlines, or turn to any news channel or get onto any social media site...What do you get more of? Good news or bad news?

Word-of-mouth advertising is the most powerful form of advertising in the world. And this is what you as a Professional need to keep in mind!

Remember- there are only 3 entrances to any business….

The Front Door!
The Telephone!
The Internet!

…And if either of these are NOT handled well, you have LOST your Customer forever!

And in some businesses, this figure can be very high. And remember women are great INFLUENCERS!

A survey carried out on **"Why customers quit"** found the following:
3% move away
5% develop other friendships
9% leave for competitive reasons
14% are dissatisfied with the product
*68% quit **because of an attitude** of indifference toward the customer by the owner, manager or some employee.*
(With the total showing 99%, you could be wondering what happened to that 1%- Well, because of the death of some of them!)

If you do a little calculation, you will find that a good over 90% is well within your control of turning this around as a Sales Professional.

Studies show that increasing customer retention rates by just 5% will increase profits anywhere from 25% to 95%, depending on the business you are in.

And remember that your customers won't love you if you give poor service, but your competitors will certainly love you!

Every time a Customer complains you need to look at this **'Complaint as a Gift'**!

Unfortunately, what often happens is that the front line employees who receive complaints take them personally or blame others. As a result, they over-react and become defensive.

To overcome this kind of reaction, it can help to think of the complaint as a genuine desire to solve the problem by someone who has taken the time and the trouble to visit, write or telephone.

A chance to set things right! And probably, the <u>only</u> chance!

How many times you would have experienced that all that the customer really wanted when he complained was an acknowledgement of the problem, an apology, an explanation and a solution to the problem. And the solution offered could have been just a refund, a replacement, an upgrade or just a hearing!

By complaining, customers are giving you several opportunities like:

- Helping you find out what you need to do to improve your systems and procedures

- See your service from the customer's point of view and try to make changes- He is the spokesperson for the many others that do not open up.

- Identify areas where your company could train your staff.

- Help you identify new products/ services/ opportunities which the market may require from you. (This is free information that you can get!)

- When customers share their story, they're not just sharing pain points. They're actually teaching you how to make your product, service, and business better.

So it is important to know what your Customers want!

All callers want **C.A.S.H.**

> **C**onvenience (at theirs, not yours!)
> **A**ction (not just lip service!)
> **S**peed (Everyone wants an answer immediately/ early/ now!)
> **H**assle-free (Not being shunted from one department to another!)

Among B2B decision makers, lack of speed in interactions with their suppliers is the number one pain point, mentioned twice as often as price.

When it comes to making a purchase, 64% of people find customer experience more important than price.

So what are some of the Pre-requisites for handling complaints?

-Top Management to have the 'Right Attitude' (as this attitude very soon percolates down- knowing what is done, is what the organization rewards)

-The 'Right Attitude' and behavior of people receiving the complaints

-Strong Systems, Policies and Procedures (Not just Smiles!)

There are eight main stages to Handling Complaints:

1. **Listen and stay calm**: Aim to diffuse the customer's feelings and clarify the exact nature of the problem.

2. **Sympathize**: This means sympathizing with the fact that the person has a problem, not accepting any blame (as you yet have not heard both sides of the case).

3. **Don't justify, argue, make excuses, interrupt or pass the buck**: Just stick to the facts, keep off what happened in the past and focus on what is going to happen now.

4. **Ask probing questions to verify facts**: This will give you more detailed information about the specific complaint and allow you to see a way through to a possible solution to the problem

5. **Check back your understanding**: Reconfirm or paraphrase what you heard.

6. **Agree a course of action and timeframe**: It is essential to find a solution which is satisfactory for the customer and from your organization's point of view.

7. **Thank them**

8. **Check the course of action is carried out:** If you agree with the customer that something will happen by a certain date, you must check that it has in fact happened. If it hasn't, you must take action to avoid making the problem even more serious.

The Things That Customers Want!

Various researches have identified a number of factors that seem to influence customers' decision to remain loyal.

- *You keep your promises*
- *You are willing to help*
- *You inspire confidence*
- *You treat customers as individuals*
- *You make it easy for customers to do business with you.*
- *All the physical aspects of your product or service give a favorable impression.*

In Closing, let me just give you the Key that is summed up in one word: **C.A.R.E:**

Customers
Are
Really
Everything!

TAKING THIS FORWARD!

What's the next step?

As a Professional Sales Person you would constantly need to remind yourself that Training is like Hygiene! We need to have a shower every day in order to stay fresh. So also you would need to keep yourself abreast and updated by constantly working on your Skill sets and upgrading them from time to time. Just reading a book from cover to cover will not guarantee a change in the way you work. No idea or concept is worth anything, if it cannot be applied to real situations. So applying these principles by putting them to immediate practice is the KEY!

So how do you do that?

Well here are a few tips to help you do so…

- Set Time to Practice with Role-Plays!
- Maybe an hour a week- You could do it with your colleagues or someone you trust.
- Work on perfecting one step at a time! Don't aim to excel in all steps. One step at a time!
- Do Periodic Evaluation of your Skills. See where you are today. Set a benchmark or standard to reach say in 3 months. Evaluate to see if you've moved in that direction.
- Keep this as a regular routine- Practice consistency!
- Read at least one book on Skill Development a month and observe/ study Top Performers! There are many books…today even free pdf books that one could download.
- Remember my favorite saying, (I used it at the start of this book!): *"If you continue to do what you are always doing, you will continue to get what you are always getting"*

In other words if we want something better than what we have today, we need to change our current style of working.

I do hope you've enjoyed and benefitted from this book. I thank you for your time and your desire to develop.

Should you have any Questions or any Suggestions that you'd want us to cover in a forthcoming book that can help you as well as others, feel free to write to: Training@SalesTrainingIndia.com or Training@Sales-Training.in

We wish you all Success as an Eagle Seller!

Gerard Assey

BIO-PROFILE OF THE AUTHOR: 'GERARD ASSEY'

Gerard Assey is a Graduate in Economics, a PGD in Management (HRD) and holds a Doctorate in Leadership. Gerard holds several International Qualifications in Sales, Debt Collection, Training & Teaching, and is a 'Fellow' of the prestigious 'Institute of Sales & Marketing Management'-UK, a Certified NLP Practitioner, a 'Certified Trainer', an 'Accredited Management Teacher-Behavioral Sciences', a 'Certified Competency Facilitator' and a 'Certified Management Consultant'- (the International credentials of a professional management consultant, awarded in accordance with global standards of the ICMCI); He is also a Member of the 'National Association of Sales Professionals' & a Member of the 'Institute of Management Consultants' backed with several years experience in varied industries, both in India and Overseas. He also holds an 'Etiquette Consultant' Certification from the USA (by Sue Fox, Author of Best Seller: 'Business Etiquette for Dummies'. She has trained some of the top celebrities' world over). He was also a recipient of a scholarship for extensive training in Japan on 'Corporate Management for India'.

Gerard Assey is 'Founder & Chief Corporate Trainer' of the Group: **'Citius, Altius, Fortius Unlimited'**- an organization that **celebrated 15 years of Glorious Service** in 2016, focusing on 3 Core Competencies: People. Performance. Profit; in functional areas of Sales & Marketing, HR & Organizational Development, covering Recruitment, Training & Consultancy!

Having managed organizations with large Sales Forces in India & Overseas, his specialization is naturally in the area of Sales Training (All levels - Presentation, Negotiation, Key/ Strategic Accounts Management & Managerial Skills for all sectors), Bid Proposal/ Capture Planning/ Management Trainings, Retail Sales, Customer Service & Customer Retention Programs, Training for Prevention & Collection of Debt, Self & Personal Development Programs (Time Management, Teamwork & Team Building, Business Etiquette & Personal Grooming, Leadership & Managerial Skills, People Management Skills, Train-the-Trainer etc), including preparation of Custom-designed Business Manuals for Internal (HR, Induction, and Sales etc) & External use (Instruction, User Manuals).

Gerard has successfully conducted over 4500 Trainings & Workshops all across India, Middle East, Africa, Europe & S.E. Asia. Besides public programs conducted regularly, both in India & Overseas, he has some of the top names as clients whom he services from Single Owners to large Public & Government undertakings, covering all sectors, for their in-house needs.

His website: www.CollectionSkills.com is the only one in this part of the world to be featured in the 'Collections & Credit Risk Magazine-USA' under 'Who's Who in Training' and ranks TOP, along with websites www.SalesTrainingIndia.com, & www.RetailSalesTraining.in today on most search engines.

Gerard is author of several published books, some of them being: 'BITE-SIZED BITS ON COMMON SENSE MANAGEMENT', 'HOW TO BECOME A SUCCESSFUL MANAGER' & 'HEART to HEART on Life's Principles' besides regularly contributing to business & trade journals, including international ones such as the 'Creative Training Techniques' and the 'Sales News' of the U.S.A. He is also a member of several prestigious bodies & trade associations, having participated in many Conferences & Workshops in India & Overseas.

Prior to his last assignment of leading & managing a large MNC as head, Gerard had a 3-year stint in the Middle East as a Consultant with a leading British Consultancy Firm.

As the past 'Official Country Representative' for the International Business Award- 'THE STEVIES'-(the business world's own Oscar) for about 4 years-he ensured a few Indian companies that qualify for the same every year!

Gerard can be contacted at:
E: mail: training@Sales-Training.in
        training@CollectionSkills.com

Websites:
        www.Sales-Training.in
        www.EtiquetteWorks.in
        www.CollectionSkills.com
        www.RetailSalesTraining.in
        www.SalesTrainingIndia.com
        www.ManualPreparation.com
        www.TrainingWithPuppets.com
        www.FirstContactAcademy.com
        www.SalesAndMarketingRecruiter.com